PENGUIN BOOKS

ON TEACHING AND WRITING FICTION

Wallace Stegner (1909–1993) was the author of, among other novels, *Remembering Laughter* (1937); *The Big Rock Candy Mountain* (1943); *Joe Hill* (1950); *All the Little Live Things* (1967, Commonwealth Club Gold Medal); *A Shooting Star* (1961); *Angle of Repose* (1971, Pulitzer Prize); *The Spector Bird* (1976, National Book Award in 1977); *Recapitulation* (1979); and *Crossing to Safety* (1987). His nonfiction includes *Beyond the Hundredth Meridian* (1954); *Wolf Willow* (1963); *The Sound of Mountain Water* (essays, 1969); *The Uneasy Chair: A Biography of Bernard DeVoto* (1974); and *Where the Bluebird Sings to the Lemonade Springs: Living and Writing in the West* (1992). Three of his short stories have won O. Henry Prizes, and in 1980 he received the Robert Kirsch Award from the *Los Angeles Times* for his lifetime literary achievements. His *Collected Stories* was published in 1990.

Lynn Stegner is the author of two novels, *Undertow* (1993) and *Fata Morgana* (1995), both nominated for the National Book Award, and a novella triptych, *Pipers at the Gates of Dawn* (2000), which won the Faulkner Society Gold Medal. She has been the recipient of a National Endowment for the Arts Writing Fellowship and a Fulbright Scholarship to Ireland. She lives with her husband, the writer Page Stegner, and her daughter, Allison, dividing her time between Vermont and California.

WALLACE STEGNER

ON
TEACHING
AND WRITING
FICTION

EDITED AND WITH A FOREWORD BY

LYNN STEGNER

PENGUIN BOOKS

PENGUIN BOOKS

Published by the Penguin Group

Penguin Putnam Inc., 375 Hudson Street, New York, New York 10014, U.S.A.

Penguin Books Ltd, 80 Strand,
London WC2R 0RL, England

Penguin Books Australia Ltd, 250 Camberwell Road,
Camberwell, Victoria 3124, Australia

Penguin Books Canada Ltd, 10 Alcorn Avenue,
Toronto, Ontario, Canada M4V 3B2

Penguin Books India (P) Ltd, 11 Community Centre,
Panchsheel Park, New Delhi – 110 017, India

Penguin Books (N.Z.) Ltd, Cnr Rosedale and Airborne Roads,
Albany, Auckland, New Zealand

Penguin Books (South Africa) (Pty) Ltd, 24 Sturdee Avenue,
Rosebank, Johannesburg 2196, South Africa

Penguin Books Ltd, Registered Offices:
Harmondsworth, Middlesex, England

First published in Penguin Books 2002

1   3   5   7   9   10   8   6   4   2

LIBRARY OF CONGRESS CATALOGING-IN-PUBLICATION DATA
Stegner, Wallace Earle, 1909–
On teaching and writing fiction / Wallace Stegner ;
edited and with a foreword by Lynn Stegner.
p.   cm.
ISBN 0-14-200147-3
1. Fiction—Authorship. 2. Fiction—Study and teaching.
I. Stegner, Lynn. II. Title.
PN3355 .S76 2002
808.3—dc21   2002028993

Printed in the United States of America
Set in Walbaum MT
Designed by M. Paul

ACKNOWLEDGMENTS

"Fiction: A Lens on Life," "To a Young Writer," and "Good-bye to all T—t!" from *One Way to Spell Man* by Wallace Stegner (Doubleday, 1982). "Fiction: A Lens on Life" first appeared in *Saturday Review*. By permission of the Estate of Wallace Stegner.

"On the Teaching of Creative Writing: Responses to a Series of Questions" edited by Edward Connery Lathem, Montgomery Endowment, Dartmouth College, 1988. Copyright © 1988 by Wallace Stegner. By permission of the Estate of Wallace Stegner. This work is based upon and extends from tape-recorded discussions that Wallace Stegner engaged in with Professors Jay L. Parini and A. B. Paulson and with visiting author, Ishmael Reed, before a Dartmouth College audience during his period in residence at the College as a Montgomery Fellow in June and July of 1980.

"Goin' to Town" from *The Big Rock Candy Mountain* by Wallace Stegner. Originally appeared in *The Atlantic Monthly*. Copyright 1938, 1940, 1942, 1943 by Wallace Stegner. Used by permission of Doubleday, a division of Random House, Inc.

All other materials are from manuscripts in the Wallace Stegner archives.

CONTENTS

FOREWORD

LET US IMAGINE a student of today entering Stanford's Writing Program; Wallace Stegner is still alive and directing the program, and our student—say, an eager fellow from Kansas hoping to maximize his educational opportunities (not to mention his parents' investment)—decides to conduct some pre-course background research on his prospective mentor. What if the guy is a postmodern fabulist by way of deconstructionism bent on squeezing the life from The Story? Or someone who spends his time writing obscure monographs on "emergent models of fiction," "comparative linguistic programming and the neoteric text," and other such ultra-refinements of academe? This would not do for our young man from Kansas who simply wants to write good fiction.

In the library computer cataloguing system he discovers screen after screen of Stegner publications, over thirty-five books, five dozen short stories, hundreds of articles, contributions, books edited, foreworded, introduced, critically examined—and our zealous pupil is sent pinballing his way from fiction to history to biography to conservation to sociology, even to religion. Wallace Stegner, he realizes, is the literary equivalent of one-stop shopping, and the education this

Kansan might receive just from reading Wallace Stegner begins to resemble what used to be the aim of higher education—a Renaissance Man.

"A fiction writer has to be a jack of all knowledges," Stegner says in one of his essays. He is "a citizen of the culture." Despite significant journeys into other fields of inquiry, despite the quality and originality of his scholarship, particularly in the study of Western history and conservation, despite his many ancillary involvements, fiction remained Stegner's first-born and favorite son. The uncovered or discovered truth would always be more compelling than the given facts, for reality, as he has said, "waits to be civilized into fiction." Of the hundreds of thousands of pages Stegner produced during his lifetime, from first, to fifteenth, to final drafts (because he was, above all else, a believer in revision), fewer than two hundred pages concern the art of fiction, and even fewer address directly creative writing as a communicable craft.

Among artists this reticence is probably not uncommon. And there may be fairly obvious explanations, not the least of which is that working artists seldom take the time, or feel the inclination, or finally possess the ability to communicate how they do what they do. Imagine Beethoven, completely deaf by his mid-fifties, trying to explain how he first *heard* the *Missa Solemnis* that he later composed. For some, part of the creative mystery lies deep within the moat of silence surrounding the work, the very incapacity to articulate its dimensions and traits providing protection; for others, talking about it poses very real danger, gusts of wind in card houses. Minimally, it seems an insult, like a heathen's lumbering footsteps through a place of private worship. For writers as a subgroup, reluctance may be intensified by the deeply personal and experiential synapse between their lives and the subjects of their books, so that any examination of the process conjures visions of stripping down in the cold light of the schoolyard.

But Wallace Stegner could not help being a teacher—by necessity (most writers need day jobs); by nature, according to the tenet that a curious man, in teaching himself, teaches others; and perhaps most of all by conviction, for he was committed to the course of revision, from the large modifications of our species and our society down to our individual selves, our ten-page narratives, our letters to the editor. "Any work of art is the product of a total human being," he has said; good fiction is "dramatized belief." To that end, Stegner and his work coevolved, the one introducing change to the other, and it in turn responding, improving, perfecting—generating the next step. "What we write," he says in " 'Goin' to Town': An Object Lesson," "is likely to be as frivolous or as serious as our lives are." Unlike many writers who blow their creative wad on an early novel (or novels), then spend the rest of their professional lives laboring against a colossal writer's block, maybe a dozen years later sweating out the long-awaited sequel to the initial success, Stegner's work matured book by book, brick by brick, so that the fully gathered force and scope of his efforts over time amounted to a literary megalopolis.

The often-quoted opening line of Cyril Connolly's *The Unquiet Grave* asserts that "the true function of a writer is to produce a masterpiece." A high pure note, to be sure, and one that no doubt has called many writers to adjust their instruments to greater purposes. But a Stegner revision of Connolly might read, *A writer must aim to be the sort of man from whom a masterpiece is possible.* A minor, and not-so-minor, adjustment. He would not have meant by this that one should preciously nourish (read *coddle*) one's talent, or rigidly safeguard (read *selfishly insist upon*) one's work time; he would have meant one must identify one's responsibilities as a citizen, as a man or a woman, and let everything, including art, proceed from there. Stegner tried determinedly to be that kind of man, striving for conduct, not merely behavior, and nowhere is this attitude more evident, more available to his readers, than in these essays and interviews on the subject closest to his heart—fiction writing.

Wallace Stegner taught first at Utah, then at Wisconsin, Harvard, and Stanford, where in 1945 he founded and directed the Stanford Writing Program until his early retirement ("I quit") in 1971. The program was modeled on what he had encountered as a student at Iowa—the only graduate writing program in the country at the time—as well as his teaching at the Bread Loaf Writers' Conference and at Harvard. It was, and is, based upon the workshop format in which Stegner says he merely "managed the environment." The idea was to create "an atmosphere of completely free inquiry." The teaching of writing, he told Richard Etulain, "is a very Socratic kind of teaching, and you should stay out of the people's way rather than get in it." He believed in what Keats called *negative capability*, both as a fictionist and as a teacher—the ability, the *necessity*, to subtract himself, his tastes, his personal opinions and prejudices, even when a

character in one of his novels or a student in one of his workshops diverged radically from a world he felt he could value.
He was there to help students realize the full literary potential in their work *through* themselves as unique and uniquely
evolving individuals, not to convert them to Stegner's style
or Stegner's themes, or even to Stegner's dreams *for* them.
Guidance, not influence, was his watchword.

"We were not quite teachers, they were not quite students," Stegner says in the introduction to *Twenty Years of
Stanford Short Stories.* Former students have described him
variously as unpretentious, nonintrusive, professional, practical, reticent, humane, polite, tough, compassionate, respect-
ful, wise, rigorously moral. Edward Abbey called him "the
only living American worthy of the Nobel Prize in literature." And Ken Kesey, when asked about his experience in
Wallace Stegner's writing workshop seminars, replied: "It
was like playing football under Vince Lombardi." From
Kesey that may have been a mixed compliment reflecting
mixed emotions—they had a civilly disputatious relationship—but one thing is clear from this remark: Kesey obviously regarded Stegner as iconic, and nothing in the record
contradicts that view. Wallace Stegner, with less than a hand-
ful of others, essentially invented creative writing as a field
of study within the Academy, and from the 1940s on, similar, frequently imitative, programs sprang up all over the
country.

How important and how vastly altered the picture becomes with these minor adjustments in orientation: Stegner
encouraged his students to write, not to think of themselves
as "writers," perhaps so that they would maintain humility

before the task at hand, or perhaps only so that the emphasis would always be on the verb *write*, on action and not on the mortmain of names or titles prematurely assumed. There is nothing more deadly to a writer than the notion that he or she has "arrived." And as Stegner himself once said, "Talents are as numerous as salmon eggs, and for the same reason: those that can survive to maturity will be few." No wonder when Richard Etulain asked him, "What is it that western writers will have to do to produce a crop of distinguished novels?" Stegner replied, "Write good books."

A great many of Stegner's students went on to do just that—write good books: Ernest Gaines, Edward Abbey, Harriet Doerr, Robert Stone, Tillie Olsen, Scott Momaday, Raymond Carver, Judith Rascoe, Wendell Berry, Max Apple, Charlotte Painter, Eugene Burdick, Scott Turow, Tom McGuane, Pat Zelver, Evan Connell, Larry McMurtry, Jim Houston, Ken Kesey, Ed McClanahan, Peter Beagle, Al Young. . . . "I try not to take credit for any of that," Stegner told Etulain. And, of course, in the grand sense he shouldn't. Yet, at the properly oblique angle, mindful of his reluctance to assume disproportionate consequence in the work of his students, and of the talents and efforts and hardships of each of these now contemporary writers, one must nevertheless give Wallace Stegner *some* credit, if only for setting the highest of examples.

This collection of articles and interviews—some previously published, some recently discovered, "a cache" as it instantly became known—will be immensely useful to anyone preparing to answer the enormity of the calling: to write truthfully of the human condition, or to help others learn to do the same. And this book will thoroughly engage anyone who sees himself as a small critical player in the evolution of our culture and species, because it asks how to live decently, responsibly, consciously, in a world that needs decent, responsible, awake citizens. As Stegner often said, paraphrasing Henry Adams, "If chaos is indeed the law of nature, then order *must* be the dream of man, and the best of all orders is art."

To be someone from whom a masterpiece is possible, one must, at last, *be* a master. Listen, say, to Ansel Adams defending Pure Photography in his rebuttal to Mr. Mortensen; or Wynton Marsalis speaking to children about Jazz, in which he makes simple sweeping connections that so transcend the music he may just as well be talking about Zen, or Rilke, or the sublimity of stone; or Jack Nicklaus talking about foot action during the golf swing; or van Gogh affirming the importance of a blade of grass over the antics of Bismarck; or the nameless physicist of the '40s explaining that the finest antigravity machine he knows of is the floor upon which he stands; or listen to Wallace Stegner talking about the writing of fiction. They are all different . . . yet all the same. To hear these masters speak, each from the very center of his subject, is to hear the intensely pure and strangely peaceful spirit at the eye of the human storm.

LYNN STEGNER
Greensboro, Vermont
September 2001

On
Teaching
and Writing
Fiction

FICTION:
A LENS ON LIFE

THE EDITOR OF A MASS-CIRCULATION MAGAZINE once told me proudly that all through the Depression he had published not one story dealing with the Depression's peculiar problems. No unemployment, no flophouses, no breadlines, no despair. Nonfiction articles by the dozen dealt with these things, but stories and serials, no. Fiction was for fun, not for illumination. Fiction was phenobarbital, not amphetamine. And even "quality" magazines, which presumably have other views of fiction, are not entirely uninfluenced by considerations of escape. I have known such a magazine, one of the best published in the United States, to refuse a story that every editor on the staff was enthusiastic about, and to refuse it only because it dealt with a woman dying of cancer. The magazine's audience contained a good many elderly women, and fiction should not touch their fears.

The kind of fiction which, approvingly or otherwise, may be called lies is outside the present discussion. It is fiction as truth that I am concerned with here, fiction that reflects experience instead of escaping it, that stimulates instead of deadening. Serious fiction, so called, is written by a different kind of writer and for a different audience. It differs in intention, in materials, in method, and in its final effect. If it entertains—as it must—it entertains at a higher intellectual and emotional level; if it deals in make-believe—as it likewise must—it creates a make-believe world in order to comment on the real one. Serious fiction is not necessarily great and not even necessarily literature, because the talents of its practitioners may not be as dependable as their intentions. But a literature, including the great, will be written in this spirit.

The difference between the writer of serious fiction and the writer of escape entertainment is the clear difference between the artist and the craftsman. The one has the privilege and the faculty of original design; the other does not. The man who works from blueprints is a thoroughly respectable character, but he is of another order from the man who makes the blueprints in the first place.

The word "artist" is not a word I like. It has been adopted by crackpots and abused by pretenders and debased by people with talent but no humility. In its capital-A form it is the hallmark of that peculiarly repulsive sin of arrogance by which some practitioners of the arts retaliate for public neglect or compensate for personal inadequacy. I use it here only because there is no other word for the serious "maker" in words or stone or sound or colors.

Joseph Conrad once outlined the qualifications for the serious artist in a little essay called simply "Books." He said:

> A novelist who would think himself of a superior essence to other men would miss the first condition of his calling. To have the gift of words is no such great matter. A man furnished with

a long-range weapon does not become a hunter or a warrior by the mere possession of a firearm; many other qualities of character and temperament are necessary to make him either one or the other. Of him from whose armoury of phrases one in a hundred thousand may perhaps hit the far-distant and elusive mark of art I would ask that in his dealings with mankind he should be capable of giving a tender recognition to their obscure virtues. I would not have him impatient with their small failings and scornful of their errors. I would not have him expect too much gratitude from that humanity whose fate, as illustrated in individuals, it is open to him to depict as ridiculous or terrible. I would wish him to look with a large forgiveness at men's ideas and prejudices, which are by no means the outcome of malevolence, but depend on their education, their social status, even their professions. . . . I would wish him to enlarge his sympathies by patient and loving observation while he grows in mental power. It is in the impartial practice of life, if anywhere, that the promise of perfection for his art can be found, rather than in the absurd formulas trying to prescribe this or that particular method of technique or conception. Let him mature the strength of his imagination among the things of this earth. . . .

It is the job of this serious artist to bring order where no order was before him or at least where his own special kind of order was not. He has for material the whole of his experience, actual and vicarious, and the wider and deeper it is, the better. The more it has hurt him, short of actual crippling, the better. The more he has enjoyed it, the better. But this experience by which he estimates the experience of men at large is always disorderly and contradictory and in our

times is apt to be an utter chaos. What he does to it is to
shape it in patterns of words that are idea and image and
character. Somewhere in the morass of his world he tramples
out a foothold, or, to change the figure, he bounds the
panoramic and bewildering view with his squared hands.
The most inclusive vision is not necessarily his aim; it is the
clearest vision he is after, and this may involve squinting or
shutting one eye or even bending over and looking at the
view upside down through his spraddled legs, Japanese fashion. However he does it—and his method is his own business—he tries with every piece of fiction, even the slightest
short story, to "create a world." The phrase is Conrad's, the
job is the endlessly repeated and endlessly new job of every
serious writer. Every piece of fiction is thus not the application of a formula, not a neat and workmanlike job of joining
and fitting, not an exercise in cleverness, but a trial of the
writer's whole understanding and a reflection of his whole
feeling and knowing.

Because he writes fiction in order to reflect or illuminate
life, his materials obviously must come out of life. These materials are people, places, things—especially people. If fiction
isn't people it is nothing, and so any fiction writer is obligated
to be to some degree a lover of his fellowmen, though he
may, like the Mormon preacher, love some of them a damn
sight better than others. The people of his stories and novels
will be, inevitably but in altered shapes, the people he himself has known. The flimsy little protestations that mark the
front gate of every novel, the solemn statements that any
resemblance to real persons living or dead is entirely coin-
cidental, are fraudulent every time. A writer has no other

material to make his people from than the people of his experience. If there is no resemblance to any real person, living or dead, the character is going to be pretty unconvincing. The only thing the writer can do is to recombine parts, suppress some characteristics and emphasize others, put two or three people into one fictional character, and pray the real-life prototypes won't sue.

The fiction writer is an incorrigible lover of concrete *things*. He has to build fiction out of such materials as the hard knotting of anger in the solar plexus, the hollowness of a night street, the sound of poplar leaves. In a contentious preface to a World War II Italian novel, Ernest Hemingway put it for the whole tribe:

> A writer finds rain [by which he means reality] to be made of knowledge, experience, wine, bread, oil, salt, vinegar, bed, early mornings, nights, days, the sea, men, women, dogs, beloved motor cars, bicycles, hills and valleys, the appearance and disappearance of trains on straight and curved tracks . . . cock grouse drumming on a basswood log, the smell of sweet grass and fresh smoked leather and Sicily.

By his very profession, a serious fiction writer is a vendor of the sensuous particulars of life, a perceiver and handler of things. His most valuable tools are his senses and his memory; what happens in his mind is primarily pictures. He is not ordinarily or ideally a generalizer, not a dealer in concepts, though some writers have tried to intellectualize fiction in this way under the impression that they were making it more respectable.

Ideas, of course, have a place in fiction, and any writer of fiction needs a mind. But ideas are not the best *subject matter* for fiction. They do not dramatize well. They are, rather, a by-product, something the reader himself is led to formulate after watching the story unfold. The ideas, the generalizations, ought to be implicit in the selection and arrangement of the people and places and actions. They ought to haunt a piece of fiction as a ghost flits past an attic window after dark.

Any good serious fiction is collected out of reality, and its parts ought to be vivid and true to fact and to observation. The parts are reassembled in such a way that the architecture, the shape of the action, is meaningful. And if the fiction is good enough, that meaning will stretch, the building will throw a shadow longer than itself, the particular will become representative, general, symbolic, indefinitely applicable to other people, other situations. The writer's meaning is thus not a single or inert thing. It expands, it becomes part of the living thought of its readers. And it is this capacity for generalized meaning that gives serious fiction its illuminating and liberating effect. But no fiction should be asked to state its meaning flatly, in conceptual terms, any more than a ghost should be called upon to come out and stand a physical examination.

The methods a writer uses to arrive at this kind of meaning are relatively unimportant except to himself. Different writers will always get their foothold in reality in different ways, different places. Every generation finds its own way of speaking out, says Gertrude Stein. No classic looks anything like any classic that has preceded it, says Hemingway. The important writer will be recognizable not by new materials but by new insights, says V. S. Pritchett.

It is often necessary for a writer to distort the particulars of experience in order to see them better. As was remarked earlier, he can look upside down or squint or put on gauze spectacles or do what he chooses, so long as his method lets him see at least part of his world more clearly. To take only one example, the padded nightmare world of Franz Kafka represents a new insight. The solemnly logical course of the incredible begets a new satire and a new humor, and for all its strangeness Kafka's fiction reflects real men and real institutions better than many more-representational kinds of fiction.

Whatever the method, it will involve a simplification. By inexorable necessity, all art simplifies. Hemingway, learning to write "beginning with the simplest things," stripping his vocabulary to the bare Anglo-Saxon, reducing his sentences to the simple declarative, eliminating all Latinate complexity, and trying to eliminate even such customary "cheating" as metaphor, simplifying his people and simplifying his themes, peeling down even his favorite theme of death to its simplest and most violent forms, represents only one kind, an extreme kind, of artistic simplification. The world that results in Hemingway's fiction may not be a world we like, but it is unmistakably a world. Conrad's world, in its own way, is just as simplified. Often it is a world within one ship, its deck the whole earth and its crew all mankind, and the moral universe bending over the actions of his people as close or as remote as the stars at sea. Even Henry James, on the surface one of the most complex and hairsplitting and qualifying

and entangled of fictionists, begins with absolutely sweeping
simplifications. To clear the way for the unimpeded moral
choices which form the crucial moments of all his stories, he
first eliminates most of what some other novelists might
build their whole books from. No James character ever has to
worry about making a living; James endows them all with
handy inheritances. No James character is fettered by family
responsibilities or any of the complex nets that fasten about
the feet of people in life. All of James's people are free to
move at will through the world he has made for them, absolutely and deliberately set free from all mundane entangle-
ments so that their moral choices can be "pure" and
uninfluenced. And though the complexities of the actual
choice, the backing and filling, the delicate hesitancies and
withholdings, the partial renunciations and the hair-fine
scruples, may be almost maddeningly complex, the act of
simplification which has made this complexity possible is
just as impressive.

Any simplification the artist chooses is legitimate; it can
be judged only on pragmatic grounds, by its success. Every
writer is a blind man feeling the elephant, and even a great
writer is likely to be limited in what he understands. His fictional world will reflect the special understandings he has.
The world of Chekhov, in which unhappy people walk grey,
muddy roads or ferry exiles like themselves across leaden
Siberian rivers or take a moment's wry enjoyment from a
wistful and frustrated life, is valid and recognizable; so is the
world Tom Lea creates in *The Brave Bulls*, where man's con-
frontation of the immortal Terror takes the shape of the rit-
ualized spectacle of a bullfight. In *The Sheltering Sky*, Paul

Bowles obtains his essential simplification by an act of arbitrary violence, putting down a pair of New York sophisticates in the primitive Sahara. The act is precisely like the act of putting a smear of culture on a slide for inspection under the microscope.

Certainly no writer can see or know all or get all life into his fiction. His quality will be measured by the amount he does succeed in getting without blurring the edges of his simplifying frame. It is the frame, the limitation, that produces for the reader the limited field of vision that can be seen under an intense light and in sharpened focus.

The effect of reading fiction conceived and executed on such terms should be an enlarged understanding. But one element of this enlarged understanding which is too often overlooked is something I can call only "intense acquaintance." In all our wandering through real or fictional worlds it is probably ourselves we seek, and since that encounter is impossible we want the next-best thing: the completely intimate contact which may show us another like ourselves. I am willing if necessary to risk condemnation as an advocate of what C. S. Lewis has called the "personal heresy," though it is certainly no such biographical hunger as Mr. Lewis deplores that I speak of here. It is utterly irrelevant that Milton misused his daughters or that Conrad had a habit of flipping bread pellets around the dinner table. What is relevant is the artist himself, or his refined and distilled spirit, the totality of his understanding. Acquaintance on that level is a thing found very rarely in life, but a book which has profoundly and intensely moved us is a most intimate experience, perhaps more intimate than marriage and more revealing than fifty years of friendship. We can make closer contact in fiction than in reality; more surely than we know the secrets of our friends, we know how this writer who is something like ourselves looks upon himself, how he fronts his life, how he, another waif in a bewildering world, has made out to survive and perhaps be at peace.

Ultimately, I am convinced, he is what we read for. The work of art is not a gem, as some schools of criticism would insist, but truly a lens. We look through it for the purified and honestly offered spirit of the artist. The ghosts of meaning that flit past the windows of his fictional house wear his face. And the reward of a lifetime of reading is a rich acquaintanceship with those gentle or powerful or rebellious or acceptant, those greatly mixed and humanly various but always greatly human ghosts.

CREATIVE WRITING

THE TERM "CREATIVE WRITING" offends some people; they think it has something affected or precious about it. Actually it is an innocent phrase developed in American schools and colleges sometime between the two world wars to designate that kind of writing *course* which is not Freshman English or Report Writing for Engineers. One suspects that "creative writing" courses grew up partly because ordinary courses in composition had got bogged down in "correctness," gentility, and the handbook-and-exercise method, and some means had to be found to free students for the development of their natural interest and delight in language. But that is beside the point here. We need only define.

Creative writing means imaginative writing, writing as an art, what the French call *belles lettres.* It has nothing to do with information or the more routine forms of communication, though it uses many of the same skills. A novel may contain a great deal of sociological or political or psychological information, and scholars may study it for that information as Freud studied literature for recorded dreams and archetypal emotional states, but information is not what any true novel is written to communicate. Like all other forms of

creative writing it is written to produce in its reader the
pleasure of an aesthetic experience, to offer him an imaginative recreation or reflection or imitation of action, thought,
and feeling. It attempts to uncover form and meaning in the
welter of love, hate, violence, tedium, habit, and brute fact
that we flounder through from day to day.

The novelist and short story writer John Cheever, when
asked why he wrote, did not say, "To show how the upper
middle class lives in Connecticut." He said, "To try to make
sense out of my life." Creative writing, whether it takes the
form of poem, short story, novel, play, personal essay, or even
biography or history, is sure to involve some search for meaning, some element of wonder and discovery, a degree of personal involvement in the result, that is not present for the
man who writes captions for *Look*, or who produces textbooks
or scientific articles, or who reports the police court news for
a country newspaper. These are worthy people plying respectable trades, but they follow another star and live by another law, and their readers expect only information from
them, not delight or revelation.

Part of the difference is rooted in the way a creative
writer uses language—plastically, for its color and sugges-
tiveness and power of sensuous evocation at least as much as
for its flat denotative meanings—but the difference goes
deeper than language. "To have the gift of words," Joseph
Conrad once wrote, "is no such great matter. A man fur-
nished with a long-range weapon does not become a hunter
or a warrior by the mere possession of a firearm; many other
qualities of character and temperament are necessary to
make him either one or the other." And Robert Frost, in a

similar mood, remarks that "all that can be done with words is soon told," and that poetry is "merely one more art of having something to say."

Any student with ambitions to be a literary artist is likely to have something he wants to say, something he can't keep still about, and he will probably discover for himself, somewhere along the road of his apprenticeship, that poems in which words are manipulated for their color or sound alone tinkle emptily and abstractly in the mind, and that shallow or conventional stories are exposed rather than supported by a self-conscious, "poetic," or elevated style. A mannered style is more often than not a sign that a writer *hasn't* much to say. For man and style are inseparable. A good writer is cocked and aimed like a gun; when he pulls the trigger he is not worrying about the caliber of his bullet or the special sound of the report. If he isn't a little dangerous, both to himself and others, he is not living up to his calling: a gun that clicks harmlessly on empty cartridges is hardly a gun at all, but a plaything. To live up to himself, to find what it is he must say, and to find ways of saying it, a writer must be ready to question and test anything, doubt anything, and when he knows what he believes in he must devote himself wholly. He is potentially both destroyer and victim, priest and sacrifice. And because words are a power easily abused, and because he must make himself heard against a clamor of television, radio, amusement parks, freeways, and the sounds of a civilization incessantly busy, a writer has to be both humble and assertive. Unless he can get himself noticed, he is nothing; but if he gets himself noticed by cheating, or out of mere vanity, he is less than nothing.

The prayer of anyone hoping to make himself into a writer should be "Lord, let me grow into such a man as *has* something to say! Let me be one of those that Henry James speaks of, one of those 'upon whom nothing is lost.' Let understanding and wisdom be engraved on my mind as deep as the lines of living on a wise and weathered face. Teach me to love and teach me to be humble and let me learn to respect human differences, human privacy, human dignity, human pain. And then let me find the words to say it so it can't be overlooked and can't be forgotten."

And so it does after all, especially for the learner, come back to the problems of words. Literature as art depends helplessly on the artist's control of his medium, for it is only by means of words that he can persuade us of the truth of what he says, or make us care about it. Possession of a weapon does not make a warrior or hunter, but no man is a very good warrior or hunter without one. Conrad and Frost can both disparage the gift of words because both have it, supremely. Having something to say, they find ways to say it. Language cuts clean for them, flashes into vivid pictures, stings us with rapier-touches of illumination and awareness. When Frost says that "like a piece of ice on a hot stove the poem must ride on its own melting," he compresses into a single image the whole process of artistic creation. And without his sensuously loaded language Conrad could never have realized so spectacularly the literary purpose he set himself: ". . . by the power of the written word to make you hear, to make you feel . . . before all, to make you see. That—and no more, and it is everything. If I succeed you shall find there according to your deserts: encouragement, consolation, fear, charm—all you demand—and, perhaps, also that glimpse of truth for which you have forgotten to ask."

It begins in the senses, it is done with words, its end is communicated insight. And when it is truly successful the insight is communicated to the reader with a pang, a heightened awareness, a sharpening of feeling, a sense of personal exposure, danger, involvement, enlargement. It is hard to believe that even the most intellectualized poets and novelists want their messages to come through cold. An emotional response in the reader, corresponding to an emotional charge in the writer—some passion of vision or belief—is essential, and it is very difficult to achieve. It is also the thing that, once achieved, unmistakably distinguishes the artist in words from the everyday user of words.

Speaking of his apprentice years in Paris in the early Twenties, Ernest Hemingway has said, "I was trying to write then, and I found the greatest difficulty, aside from knowing truly what you really felt, rather than what you were supposed to feel, and had been taught to feel, was to put down what really happened in action; what the actual things were which produced the emotion that you experienced. In writing for a newspaper you told what happened and, with one trick and another, you communicated the emotion aided by the element of timeliness which gives a certain emotion to any account of something that has happened on that day; but the real thing, the sequence of motion and fact which made the emotion and which would be as valid in a year or in ten years, or, with luck and if you stated it purely enough, always, was beyond me and I was working very hard to get it."

The passage suggests a simple-sounding but rigorous program of training for any beginning writer: Learn to see straight; practice, with endless patience, "stating purely" what you find to say; and see it and state it with the aim of communicating not only its meaning but its quintessential emotion, the thing that made it important to you in the first place. No course in creative writing, whether self-administered or offered by a school, could propose a better set of exercises. Such a program might preserve a young writer both from the attempt by teachers to "correct him into importance," and from the equally misguided tendency to overpraise him for anything that shows the slightest imaginative flair. If he sets himself the highest standards from the beginning, he is not likely to be misled by the standards of others.

I have said that creative writing begins in the senses. More than that, the stamp of the senses must remain on it. No one without acute senses and the willingness to use them should pretend to literature, because without senses he cannot create images, and images are his only means of making his reader hear and feel and see. By pure intelligence he can out-argue a reader, convince him, sway him to ideas, but for the creative writer intelligence must be supplemented by the equipment of sensuousness. A creative writer not only perceives in images, he must communicate in them, and the reader must read in them. They are both source and method. An image is crystallized by the perceptions of the writer, is converted into words like a cable message being scrambled, and finally is reconverted by the reader into something like the original perception. And as the cable message comes out clearer for the scrambling-and-unscrambling process, so the literary image the reader receives may be less confused by static than the perceptions of his own senses.

The creative writer is compulsively concrete—that is, he is bound to the *things* of experience. However strongly he holds his ideas, he cannot express them in the way a philosopher or a social scientist does. He does not deal in concepts, in formulated patterns of thought, but in *iconic* ways, in the way of images and imitations; he is concerned with people, places, actions, feelings, sensations. His fictional house should be haunted by ideas, not inhabited by them; they should flit past the windows after dark, not fill the rooms. The moment anyone tries to make poems or stories of ideas alone he is at the edge of absurdity; he can only harangue, never interest and persuade, because ideas in their conceptual state are simply not dramatic. They have to be put into the form of people and actions to achieve their proper force. One Macbeth on stage is worth a thousand essays on ambition.

Thus Shelley, speaking of so refined a concept as the Platonic Ideal, found in "Adonais" images to make the abstraction concrete and memorable:

> The One remains, the many change and pass;
> Heaven's light forever shines, earth's shadows fly;
> Life, like a dome of many-colored glass,
> Stains the white radiance of eternity.

What if he had been content to say, "The Ideal is pure and changeless, while the Real is impure and impermanent"?

Sometimes a writer begins with ideas, as Hawthorne did, and makes them into flesh and blood; sometimes he starts

with flesh and blood, as Mark Twain did, and lets flesh and
blood work themselves out *into* idea. Either way, he is
steadily called upon to render the way life feels to him or to
his imaginary characters. He must render it vividly because
he wants the reader to feel it vividly, and he therefore makes
use of all the senses he has. That is why literature overflows
with such sensuous things as the hollowness of footsteps in a
night street, the fisting of hard anger in the solar plexus, the
weight of hydrangeas brushed against the summer dark, the
look and texture of the down, fuzzy as a pussywillow, on
the back of a fair-haired woman's neck. Whether for poetry
or prose, we must be able to express—which means we must
have taken the trouble to *know*—the qualities of things, the
hardness and smoothness and splinteriness, the feel of heat
and cold, the physical symptoms of fear, delight, loss. We
must observe and be able to communicate differing qualities
of voice and gesture, the nearly invisible signs around the
eyes and mouth and in the hands and body by which we in-
terpret an individual's state of mind or emotion. We have to
be able to stimulate the sweat glands and the hair follicles,
make mouths water, turn stomachs, command tears, laughter, scorn—all with words.

Because human beings are predominantly eye-minded,
most literary images are visual—literally pictures—but they
may just as properly involve any other sense, or several at
once. Sometimes they are heavily and damply auditory, as
when Mark Twain's jumping frog leaps after a fly and alights
on the counter "as solid as a gob of mud." Sometimes they
are both visual and auditory, as in Browning's "quick sharp
scratch/And blue spurt of a lighted match." They may be

tactual, as when Keats, at the beginning of "The Eve of St. Agnes," enforces on our skins the very shrink and shudder of cold:

> St. Agnes' Eve—Ah, bitter chill it was!
> The owl, for all his feathers, was a-cold;
> The hare limped trembling through the frozen grass,
> And silent was the flock in woolly fold:
> Numb were the beadsman's fingers, while he told
> His rosary, and while his frosted breath,
> Like pious incense from a censer old,
> Seem'd taking flight for heaven, without a death,
> Past the sweet Virgin's picture, while his prayer he saith.

It is a common misconception that an image invariably involves a figure of speech. Often it does. The mystic poet Francis Thompson, speaking of a poppy as a "yawn of fire," brings a metaphor to his aid; D. H. Lawrence describing the sea and sky of a Mediterranean sunrise as opening like the two halves of a clamshell employs a simile. The Browning lines obtain their vividness from onomatopoeia, the imitation of a sound. But the Keats stanza gets its total effect of cold, which is its principal virtue, almost without figurative language: "woolly fold" (metonymy) is there as a contrast, and the simile of the frosted breath is primarily visual.

Sometimes a direct and scrupulously accurate reporting can be as vivid as any figure of speech. Young Hemingway, learning to write "beginning with the simplest things," did his best to avoid all such "cheating" as metaphor. Since all metaphorical language, without exception, involves some explicit or implicit comparison, and since a comparison is a sort of judgment, a writer aiming to be completely objective might well be suspicious of it. To say, as T. S. Eliot says,

> Let us go then, you and I,
> Where the evening is spread out against the sky
> Like a patient etherised upon a table;

is to reveal not only something of J. Alfred Prufrock's disenchantment but perhaps to reveal something of Eliot too: some wry and fastidious irony, some distaste for crude life, has been expressed in the comparison between sunset and an operating table. On the other hand, listen to Hemingway describing a trout stream in "Big Two-Hearted River":

> He watched them holding themselves with their noses into the current, many trout in deep, fast-moving water, slightly distorted as he watched far down through the glassy convex surface of the pool, its surface pushing and swelling smooth against the resistance of the log-driven piles of the bridge.

Here the author is only an eye; he makes no judgment, overt or covert. There is no metaphorical leap such as that in the Eliot lines, but only a reproduction of the thing seen. In later stories Hemingway relaxed his ban against both metaphorical language and symbolism, and rightly; to try to do without them is to write with one hand tied. Nevertheless his attempt to put the whole burden of vividness on the precision of observation was training of an invaluable kind, not unlike the training which Flaubert set for his pupil Maupassant when he sent him out to report in a single phrase or a single word the content of an action.

Whether dressed up in metaphor or stripped to the bare observation, any creative writing must be concrete, must communicate by images. Fortunately, the possible ways of seeing, the possible styles and "tones of voice," are almost as individual as our fingerprints. There are other ways than Hemingway's, other ways than Flaubert's.

"Don't forget, Scott," Thomas Wolfe wrote in a letter to F. Scott Fitzgerald, who had been badgering him about economy and form,

> don't forget that a great writer is not only a leaver-outer but also a putter-inner, and that Shakespeare and Cervantes and Dostoevsky were great putter-inners—greater putter-inners, in fact, than taker-outers and will be remembered for what they put in—remembered, I venture to say, as long as Monsieur Flaubert will be remembered for what he left out.

Wolfe himself was a mighty putter-inner; he could hardly let a character pass a hardware store window without enumerating every tool in it, and the sights and sounds of afternoon in a familiar town set him into a sensuous frenzy:

> Light came and went and came again, the great plume of the fountain pulsed and winds of April sheeted it across the Square in a rainbow gossamer of spray. The fire department horses drummed on the floors with wooden stomp, most casually, and

with dry whiskings of their clean, coarse tails. The street cars
ground into the Square from every portion of the compass and
halted briefly like wound toys in their familiar quarter-hourly
formula. A dray, hauled by a boneyard nag, rattled across the
cobbles. . . . The courthouse bell boomed out its solemn warning
of immediate three . . .

That is a passage worth study, particularly for its choice
of strong and active verbs: "pulsed," "sheeted," "drummed,"
"ground," "rattled," "boomed." But it is certainly not seven-
eighths below the surface, as Hemingway said icebergs and
stories should be. It is piled on, heaped until it runs over. Different from either method is the impressionism of such a
writer as Anton Chekhov, who said, "You will get the full effect of a moonlight night if you write that on the mill-dam a
little glowing star-point flashed from the neck of a broken
bottle, and the round, black shadow of a dog, or a wolf,
emerged and ran." In that same impressionist manner,
Stephen Crane carries us along with a horribly wounded sol-
dier walking to some quiet place to die. The whole passage is
like a prolonged, silent scream, and it ends with a single staring phrase: "The red sun was pasted in the sky like a wafer."

Still different is the symbolist way of Yeats, Eliot, Joyce,
and all its Dadaist and surrealist variations. It is not the place
to discuss them here, but it should at least be noted that these
writers deliberately conceal as much as they reveal, and that
when they do choose to make a meaning evident, they do so
by means of difficult private symbols or by means of tiny
epiphanies like those in Joyce's story, "Ivy Day in the Com-

mittee Room," where the spirit of the dead leader Parnell is brought ironically into a roomful of small-time heelers and sycophants by the almost hidden showing of the symbolic ivy leaf that was the emblem of Parnell's movement.

No young writer needs to worry whether he is going to be a naturalist, realist, romanticist, impressionist, surrealist, or anything else. The intellectual currents of his time will carry him into contact with most of them, and his own enthusiasms will lead him to follow one or another, or perhaps several in succession, before he finds his own way. Most potential writers are omnivorous readers; and in the nature of things an apprentice is sure to imitate——he has no other way to learn. And though he may try very hard to "develop a style of his own," his real style will be a good while in developing and will parallel or reflect the development of his own mind and sensibility. The best practice for finding the style that naturally fits him is to follow Hemingway's method, and simply try to state purely whatever is before his eyes.

On New England farms years ago, butter used to be put up in wooden tubs called firkins, the tub built up by successive churnings until it was full, and then taken to market. Color, quality, and sweetness were seldom uniform, and buyers used to test a firkin by running a hollow tube clear to the bottom and getting a core sample of all the layers. That is the way a young writer had better approach the selection of words.

On the surface every word means something definite, just as on the surface a firkin of butter may look uniform in color and quality. In certain of the social sciences there are periodic attempts to create a technical language with only this unchanging denotative meaning, so that words can be used with the precision of mathematical symbols. One linguist has been quoted as saying that "mathematics is the best that language can do." But every poet and novelist and essayist and playwright would dispute his remark. A pearl is a pearl, but a pearl taken from a dead oyster is worthless—it has no sheen. And the words that we value are words with sheen, the kind we cut from the living body of the language.

Nothing is so likely to let the wind out of a young writer's enthusiasm for creation as the rigid, genteel "correctness" that schools too often try to impose. We approach the student with a list of thou-shalt-nots, and sheets of bad sentences to be corrected, when we might instead get him indulging the natural—indeed the irrepressible—playfulness that people have about language. Language has been called the greatest human invention; upon it practically all human civilization is built. In spite of the exercise books and the negative approach of our schools, language stays alive; it is often more alive in the mouths of truck drivers than in the correct mouths of people who feel that there is a single proper or correct way to say everything. Emerson envied the speech of draymen. All of us have experienced occasions when some untaught and uninhibited young man, kidding a girl or coaching at third base, has struck sparks with a casual remark—has done exactly what language ought to permit him to do, communicate vividly.

This is not to say that correctness does not matter, or that there is no distinction between good usage and bad usage. It is only to say that we should be prepared, and should prepare ourselves, for growth and invention at any level of language. And the more the schools petrify our mother tongue, the more invention will have to come from the unlettered. When Hemingway remarked that "all American literature comes from one book by Mark Twain called *Huckleberry Finn*," he was exaggerating; nevertheless the inspired lingo, the common speech, of Huck Finn has had, beyond question, more effect on our literature and on the development of the American language than any other book. A single test will suffice. Read any paragraph of Hawthorne, good as he is, and hear how old-fashioned and stilted it sounds in the ear. Then read a passage of *Huckleberry Finn*, say Huck's description of a river sunrise:

> Not a sound anywheres—perfectly still—just like the whole world was asleep, only sometimes the bull-frogs a-cluttering, maybe. The first thing to see, looking away over the water, was a kind of dull line—that was the woods on t'other side; you couldn't make nothing else out; then a pale place in the sky; then more paleness spreading around; then the river softened up away off, and warn't black any more, but gray; you could see little dark spots drifting along ever so far away—trading-scows, and such things; and long black streaks—rafts; sometimes you could hear a sweep screaking; or jumbled up voices, it was so still, and sounds come so far; and by-and-by you could see a streak on the water which you know by the look of the streak that there's a snag there in a swift current which breaks on it and makes that streak look that way; and you see the mist curl

up off of the water, and the east reddens up, and the river, and you make out a log-cabin in the edge of the woods, away on the bank on t'other side of the river, being a wood-yard, likely, and piled by them cheats so you can throw a dog through it any-wheres; then the nice breeze springs up, and comes fanning you from over there, so cool and fresh and sweet to smell on account of the woods and the flowers; but sometimes not that way, be-cause they've left dead fish laying around, gars, and such, and they do get pretty rank; and next you've got the full day, and everything smiling in the sun, and the song-birds just going it!

By the handbook standard, that should be liberally marked up with red pencil; by any other standard it is mag-nificent prose. It does what language was created to do. Mark Twain has observed the scene with the greatest possible pre-cision, and he has found a way of stating it purely. That the way of stating it contains a good many barbarisms of lan-guage is irrelevant. The minor barbarisms simply do not matter; the major ones, the bull-frogs a-cluttering and the song-birds just going it and the wood-yard piled by them cheats so you can throw a dog through it anywheres, are the barbarisms of genius, the kind of inventive and playful lan-guage that we cannot afford to suppress. They crop up in our everyday life all the time, in casual speech, in popular songs, even in advertising slogans. They exist as a kind of private language in the subculture of the American adolescent; they well up out of jazz and the jazz world. A young writer would make a mistake to be enslaved to the subliterary languages of America, but he would be a fool to ignore them. The delight with which tens of thousands greeted J. D. Salinger's *Catcher in the Rye* was a delight largely of the ear: we got pleasure out of the freshness of that juvenile argot, with all the natural sound of the spoken voice in it.

For the young writer there is no rule on language, there are only warnings, and they concern the extremes of choice. Bookish and literary language, the kind that half embarrasses its author when it is read aloud, is obviously a mistake; but so is the affected overmasculine toughness that some young men adopt in the belief that it permits them to love literature without being called effeminate. Between those extremes anything that works is good, and a playful way with language is always better than a solemn one. Once at Bryce Canyon, in southern Utah, I heard a man say to his wife as they got out of their car, "Well, shall we pace over and peer at it?" At a pleasantly foolish level he was indulging a playful attitude toward words; I would expect more of him in the way of true appreciation than I would from someone who braced himself solemnly and got ready to experience the feelings he thought he should have, and looked down into the canyon for the Thunder Spirit.

Surely, for the playful writer or the writer searching for the inevitable word, there is no such thing as an exact synonym. Two firkins may look alike, but the tester reveals differences in the lower layers. In the old schoolroom example, "He wiped off her face with a damp cloth" is a very different sentence from "He swabbed off her mug with a soggy rag." The connotations of "cloth" and "rag," or of "wipe" and "swab," are very different, though denotatively they look much alike. Only the context, the purpose you have in mind, can tell you which to use.

One of the greatest strengths of English as a literary language is the great variety of choices, from Latin, French, Anglo-Saxon, Greek, and other roots, for almost any object, idea, or action we want to express. It is customary to disparage words of Latin derivation and praise the good tough curt Anglo-Saxon, but these matters are surely best left to the writer's own choice, and to the nature of what he wants to say. James Joyce begins the first story in *Dubliners* with a string of dead, flat monosyllabic words: "There was no hope for him this time: it was the third stroke," but when we praise that opening for its paralyzed appropriateness we should not rule out Shakespeare's "multitudinous seas incarnadine." The words that fit are the words to choose, and it does not matter whether they come to us from the Greeks or from a singing commercial.

In one sense, every word is a symbol. Letters on a page or a certain sound in the mouth convey a meaning to us; "tree" is four letters and a certain sound, but it is also a thing with bark and leaves. And sometimes it is more: put into a context which includes the word "Calvary" it becomes a metaphor for the cross on which Christ was nailed. That kind of extension of meaning which we call symbolism is actually one of the most suggestive and economical ways of communicating the aesthetic experience.

A road and a town are specific things, but look what they become in Housman's "To an Athlete Dying Young":

> Today, the road all runners come,
> Shoulder-high we bring you home,

> And set you at the threshold down,
>
> Townsman of a stiller town.

There the symbolism is perfectly plain, on what Professor Harry Levin of Harvard calls the conventional level. Much poetic symbolism is of this commonly accepted kind; a journey symbolizes human life, as in *Pilgrim's Progress*; the seasons suggest the ages of man, as in Shakespeare:

> That time of year thou mayst in me behold
>
> When yellow leaves, or none, or few, do hang
>
> Upon those boughs which shake against the cold,
>
> Bare ruin'd choirs, where late the sweet birds sang.

A symbolism less traditional, but still overt, is what Professor Levin calls the *explicit*: "Thou too sail on, O ship of state!" A third sort, the *implicit*, takes us into more ambiguous country. We know that Moby-Dick is more than whale, but what precisely is he? God? The Spirit of Evil? A manifestation of pure mindless Force? No single explanation will fully satisfy. It is in this ambiguous world of unexplained or private or floating meaning that much contemporary writing exists; and much contemporary criticism falls into even darker categories of symbolism, what Professor Levin calls the *conjectural* and the *inadmissible*.

Again, there is no rule for the student except that he should read, and read, and read, and fill his mind, and express it as he can. If he is sucked into the allegorical maelstrom he may go down; many have. But he is safe in the conventional and explicit levels, and reasonably safe in the implicit. When he begins using private symbols, and disguising rather than revealing his thought, he risks exclusiveness and pedantry, as Joyce risked it. One thing, however, he can be sure of: if the outward story or poem is solid, the symbolism, even though ambiguous, will take care of itself. *Gulliver's Travels*, representing far more than appears on its surface, remains a fascinating children's wonder story. *Moby-Dick* is still an adventure after a fabulous fish. It does not attempt to cast a shadow without having any solid substance.

A young writer should try everything, but some forms will come more naturally to him than others. Short lyrics, short stories, one-act plays, are more within his scope than longer forms, and he will learn most by making many beginnings and endings—the hardest parts of any piece of writing, and the places where, as Chekhov says, a man is most likely to lie.

If he chooses lyric poetry, he has no problem about how to hide himself, because the lyric is a personal, a most personal art. But if he chooses fiction, and particularly the short story, he will have to learn, like any good puppeteer, to keep his hands and feet from showing. Basic to all fictional writing is the problem of point of view, the stance or the consciousness from which one chooses to make the reader follow the story. Fiction is usually much less personal than the lyric, and less bound to objectivity than the drama. "The lyrical form," as Stephen Dedalus proposes to himself in *A Portrait of the Artist as a Young Man*, is in fact the simplest verbal vesture of an instant of emotion, a rhythmical cry such as ages ago cheered on the man who pulled at the oar or dragged stones up a slope. He who utters it is more conscious of the instant of emotion than of himself as feeling emotion.

Conversely, the artist of the dramatic form, "like the God of the creation, remains within or behind or beyond or above his handiwork, invisible, refined out of existence, indifferent, paring his fingernails." The writer of fiction, however he may pretend to be indifferent and invisible, is always there; he cannot help steering, cannot help providing some double vision, some commentary, insight, or irony. If he wants a reader to participate intensely, he adopts the point of view of one of the characters in the story, sees through those eyes alone, thinks with that mind, knows nothing that that individual would not know. If he wants to imitate the dramatic, he pretends to be a camera—a sound camera—as John Steinbeck does in *Of Mice and Men*, a story which was written to fulfill at one and the same time the requirements of a novel and those of a play. But if, as Chekhov, Conrad, Crane, and many others do, the writer wants to have the immediacy of drama but still keep the right of comment, then he has a subtle job of keeping himself out of his story while still making it say what he wants it to say.

Point of view is too complicated a subject to be more than mentioned here, but this is the area where a fiction writer's principal skill must be developed, once he has perfected his gift of words. He must be in his story but not *ap-*

parently in it; the story must go his way while appearing to act itself out. For this sort of skill, the short story is the best practice ground. It is so short that a flaw in the point of view shows up like a spider in the cream; it is so concentrated that it forces a writer to develop great economy and structural skill; and it is so intense that like a high-velocity bullet it has the knock-down power of a heavier missile.

And a writer *must* knock readers down. This is what he must constantly have in mind: to make people listen, to catch their attention, to find ways to make them hold still while he says what he so passionately wants to say. He is an ancient mariner laying hands on wedding guests, staying them with his skinny hand and his glittering eye. And though creative writing as an intellectual exercise may be pursued with profit by anyone, writing as a profession is not a job for amateurs, dilettantes, part-time thinkers, 25-watt feelers, the lazy, the insensitive, or the imitative. It is for the creative, and creativity implies both talent and hard work.

ON THE
TEACHING
OF CREATIVE
WRITING

❑ *What, Mr. Stegner, is your reply to the question of whether creative writing can, in point of fact, be "taught"?*

That question has been coming at me, as you can imagine, for a long time, because I taught writing for something like forty-four years, before retiring.

I remember a time, years ago, when I dined with the dons at Magdalen College, Oxford. They stood me up and filled me as full of arrows as St. Sebastian. I presume they all believed that writing must be learned—that it is a gift that needs developing and disciplining—but none of them believed that it is a legitimate subject for a university course.

All I could say in answer was that they lived under privileged conditions. In England, a small country the size of some American states, a young writer can go to London, frequent the right Hampstead pub, meet literary people, begin to do a few of the chores of literary journalism—a book review here, a little article there, a poem, a critical essay—and in that way begin a literary apprenticeship.

The United States is too big a country for that. New York,

in spite of the fact that it is the publishing capital, is not a literary capital, in the sense that London or Tokyo or Vienna is. Some young writers—Tom Wolfe, for an example—do throw themselves into that surf and try to swim. Others do not; many cannot.

So, for many Americans who grow up in the provinces, as I did, there is no convenient and inevitable place to go to make contact with other writers and with the writing establishment, the general technology of writing. Most regional capitals, at least until recently, have been culturally impoverished or undeveloped. The best alternative has been those minor centers that exist in colleges and universities. In the circumstances, their development has been inevitable.

Within the academy, of course, there are limited things that a teacher can do, apart from encouraging the environment of interest and criticism within which writing can take place. How can anyone "teach" writing, when he himself, as a writer, is never sure what he is doing?

Every book that anyone sets out on is a voyage of discovery that may discover nothing. Any voyager may be lost at sea, like John Cabot. Nobody can teach the geography of the undiscovered. All he can do is encourage the will to explore, plus impress upon the inexperienced a few of the dos and don'ts of voyaging.

A teacher who has been on those seas can teach certain things—equivalents of the use of compass and sextant: the language and its uses, and certain tested literary tools and techniques and strategies and stances and ways of getting at the narrative essence of a story or novel or the dramatic force of a play or the memorableness of a poetically honed thought.

Any teacher can discourage bad (meaning, unproductive or ineffective) habits and encourage those that work. He can lead a young talent to do what it is most capable of doing, and save it from some frustrating misdirections. He can communicate the necessary truth that good writing is an end in itself, that an honest writer is a member of a worthy guild. That may be the most important function of the teacher of writing.

Within the academy, which is itself a sort of monastic sanctuary in the cultural darkness, he can encourage—and perhaps create a substitute for—the places that more developed societies have created: the Mermaid Taverns and Hampstead pubs. In a university, people of similar interests and comparable talents can get together and knock sparks off each other.

In my experience, the best teaching that goes on in a college writing class is done by members of the class, upon one another. But it is not automatic, and the teacher is not unimportant. His job is to manage the environment, which may be as hard a job as for God to manage the climate.

❑ *Is it the case that everybody can be taught to be a creative writer? And should everyone be?*

No, on both counts. I have always tried to keep in mind Ring Lardner's remark that you can't make a writer out of a born druggist. You can't make a sprinter out of a 250-pound hammer-thrower or a musician out of someone who is tone deaf. You begin with a gift, big or little, and you try to help it become whatever its potential permits.

It is a fact that many people don't know their own potential, and without help will never have a glimmer of what it might be. It is a sadder fact that some misread their potential and aspire to be something which their gifts simply don't allow them to become.

Nevertheless, I believe that talent is more common than we think, that it is all over the place, and that almost everyone has some degree of it—something worth developing. That does not mean that you can count on producing writers, the way an engineering school can count on producing engineers.

Writing is not a function of intelligence or application. It is a function of gift—that which is given and not acquired. All any teacher can do is work with what is given.

But I do believe that everyone born should have a chance to become the best he is capable of and that many have undeveloped or obscured gifts that, like spores, will grow if they are given water.

❑ *What does one look for in trying to determine whether an individual has any real potentiality as a creative writer?*

One looks for signs of gift: obviously perceptiveness, alertness to the observed world, a feel for language. It is not easy, and different kinds of writers display very different stigmata of gift.

If you looked only at the feel for language, you would never predict that Theodore Dreiser, say, would become an important writer. The fact is, Dreiser had everything a novelist needs *except* the feel for language. He became an important novelist without having the ability to write an English sentence. So, prediction is a very dicey matter.

At Stanford we dealt with hundreds of applicants for fellowships. Candidates wrote a letter saying what they hoped to do, and sent along a sample of what they had done. I remember one year when I picked up two application letters together. One was full of pretension, metaphysical conceits, strained metaphors, flowers of rhetoric. It was Faulkner crossed with Tristan Tzara or Monty Python—so turgid that one strained for its meaning—and it was four pages long.

The other one was four lines long. It said only that what spoke to this candidate, in our program, was its willingness to give every talent a chance to be itself; she hoped to write stories and hoped to write them well.

The second candidate's name was Tillie Olsen, and she did write stories, and write them well. We gave her a fellowship, and did not give one to the other applicant, because what spoke to us from her letter was directness and honesty, and what spoke to us from his was pretension and self-consciousness. He wanted, terribly, to be "literary." She wanted to write stories.

Not all prediction is as easy as that, and all such decisions are harrowing to make, because they mean so much, so personally, to the people you make them about.

Ultimately, what one looks for is sensibility—which need not be as effete as it sounds—and sensibility is essentially *senses*. One looks for evidence that eyes and ears are acute and active, and that there is some capacity to find words for conveying what the senses perceive and what sense perceptions do to the mind that perceives them.

What one looks for in language is not mechanical perfection of syntax. What one looks for is accuracy, rightness, vividness. And beyond that, of course, some notion, however rudimentary, of the seriousness of good writing, some sense that literature should enhance life.

❑ *Can individuals be given tutelage in creative writing at too early an age?*

There is, surely, no age too early for the development of sensibility, and enough poets have lisped in numbers to make me believe that there is no age too young for writing.

The apprenticeship for poets is likely to be shorter than for fiction writers, because (at least in our time) poetry is essentially lyrical, which means personal, and the person is aware of himself well before he is fully aware of his entanglement in a society and a culture—the sort of entanglement out of which fiction most often arises.

So, there is no "legal age" for indulging the itch to write, but there may be a certain minimum age when one may expect the results to be memorable. Poetry matures younger than prose; individuals and sensibilities are very different.

But there may well be such a thing as *teaching* writing too early. Teaching implies a personality, in the student, that is at least half-formed. It also involves—I wish it didn't, but it does—a certain validation of the student's ego. Young writers test themselves against the opinions of others, and especially against publication. Putting something in print is an enormous maximation of the literary ego.

I have known teachers who made junior-high and high-school students offensively literary, by persuading them that what they wrote was better, more mature, more worthy than it was. They have helped encumber children of fifteen with vast expectations, sure to be disappointed or long postponed, and that seems to me an ill-service. Students that young should be encouraged and challenged; they should not be inflated with false hopes.

The literary apprenticeship, despite the contrary evidence of certain precocious individuals, is normally long. Most fiction writers are not really writers until their late twenties or even later. And the maturing process cannot be taught, it has to happen.

You can write your head off when you are in college or for a few years afterward, and people may praise what you do, but nobody is likely to want to publish it. Then, suddenly, someone does want to publish something. You can't see any difference between it and the things you were doing two or three years ago, but some editor can. You send him the earlier things, hopefully, and he sends them back. But he wants the new one, and perhaps other new ones after it. Something unpredictable has happened in your head or on your typewriter, and no teacher did it—though a teacher may have helped it along.

A long answer to a short question. A shorter answer would be: Young writers should be encouraged to write, and discouraged from thinking they are writers. If they arrive at college with literary ambitions, they should be told that everything they have done since their first childhood poems, printed in the school paper, has been preparation for entering a long, long apprenticeship.

At least in the beginning, that apprenticeship does not have to be served in a classroom. Letters can be part of it, journals, anything that will force the expression of experience in words.

❑ *Does that suggest, then, the appropriateness of urging students to gain experience with life, before they seriously attempt any pursuit of writing?*

If you have to urge a writing student to "gain experience with life," he is probably never going to be a writer. Henry James has some useful advice in this regard. He urges young writers to be people "upon whom nothing is lost." But in another essay, one on Maupassant, he is dubious about Flaubert's celebrated instruction to observe the cart horse until you can render him distinct from every other cart horse on earth.

Note-taking, James suggests (and he was himself a great note-taker, so that his advice may be ambiguous), is hardly the best way. You don't go out and "commit experience" for the sake of writing about it later; and if you have to make notes on how a thing has struck you, it probably hasn't struck you.

The people who are really going to be writers don't need urging to pay attention to their lives and experience. Experience strikes them. Even James, whom one critic describes as having proceeded through his life from inexperience to inexperience, was never in any doubt when one of his inexperiences was memorable. He was one of those upon whom nothing, even an inexperience, was lost.

Any life will provide the material for writing, if it is attended to. Willa Cather said that a novel is what happens in this room, today. I think it is. No urging is necessary. The ones who are going to do something will know what struck them.

❑ *But you yourself once declared, "Any work of art is the product of a total human being." And you have also emphasized that success in literature is not simply "a matter of mere verbal facility." Do those observations not suggest that a creative writer must possess, as background for exposition and expression, a relative maturity of experience?*

Oh, sure. Of course. I didn't mean to imply that James's inexperience was *really* inexperience or that any writer, especially a writer of fiction, can write out of his head, out of pure abstract invention. He can't *invent* without experience.

What I meant was that experience sought for the sake of writing about it may produce reporting, or travel books, but it is not likely to produce literature. And experience is of many kinds, some of them so subtle and quiet it takes a good Geiger counter to detect them.

The way to gain experience is to live, but that does not mean one must go slumming for the exotic or outrageous or adventurous or sordid or, even, unusual. Any experience, looked at steadily, is likely to be strange enough for fiction or poetry.

By the same token, the individual who has lived deeply

and widely—and I mean lived, not gone slumming or adventuring for literary purposes—has more to write about, and perhaps a better base for mature wisdom, than someone less privileged.

And yet, I don't know. What did Thoreau know? He lived deeply in Walden, deeply in books, deeply in his mind. By occupation he was nothing spectacular, part-time surveyor and handyman.

The subject of fiction is not just what one did yesterday. It may borrow from the experience of others than the author.

Robert Frost used to say that a fiction writer should be able to tell what happened to himself as if it had happened to someone else, and what happened to someone else as if it had happened to himself. That puts the emphasis where it belongs: on the technique of communication, the persuasiveness of the fiction.

❑ *In your judgment, what is it that most needs to be done for students?*

They need to be taken seriously. They need to be assured that their urge to write is legitimate. And, even when they must be discouraged from wasting their lives in a hopeless effort, they must not be dismissed flippantly—these are hearts you are treading on.

Every student has a right to be listened to and be told honestly whether what he has written strikes no sparks or few or many. Before a teacher tells anyone he is good, and has that magical promise, he had better make sure of what he is saying; before he discourages anyone, he had better remember how intimate a thing writing is and how raw the nerves that surround it.

There are no special techniques for any of this. This is part of the Socratic burden of teaching writing. It is more an attitude than a technique.

❑ *Do you consider reading to be an important part of the preparation for writing?*

Oh, definitely. Absolutely. We learn any art not from nature, but from the tradition, from those who have practiced it before. Hemingway said you can steal from anybody you're better than. But you can steal—in the sense of being influenced by and, even, improving upon—those who are better than you, too. People do it all the time.

You can hear Joyce in Dos Passos' *U.S.A.* and Dos Passos' *U.S.A.* in Mailer's *The Naked and the Dead*. Writers teach other writers how to see and hear.

The possibility that illumination will come to your mind straight from personal experience is about as likely as that a boy will show slick basketball moves without having watched or played with older boys in some playground.

Furthermore, what influences you will change with time. You begin, after all, with what your taste and intelligence and experience will permit you to begin with.

I have heard T. S. Eliot say that the way to inculcate a love for poetry is to let young people begin with what moves them, the *Lays of Ancient Rome* or some such narrative, swift, easily comprehended, and easily remembered poetry. If a youngster has let "Horatius at the Bridge" or "The Battle of Lake Regillus" work on him, he is pretty sure to go on to something harder and more rewarding—Eliot himself, perhaps, or Wallace Stevens or Rilke or whoever.

It goes without saying, too, that those who *hear* a lot of poetry in their youth are likelier to become poets than those who do not.

Though it is always helpful to the young to be steered and guided toward what may catch their interest, I would be inclined, also, to throw open the library and let them find many things for themselves. The delight of discovery is a major pleasure of reading; and discovery is one of the best ways to light a fire in a creative mind.

Imitation, of course, is a potential danger. There is commonly a stage in any writer's life when the influence of some admired writer shows. But imitation wears out fast. No talent that amounts to anything is likely to be encumbered with it long. And the talent that doesn't amount to anything can only be helped along for a certain distance, anyway.

Actually, it is remarkable how wide and varied is the reading of most of the writers I know. They read for curiosity, for the purpose of keeping an eye on the competition, for the pleasure of discovery in their own field. But they also read archaeology, biography, history, physics, geography, the revelations out of biochemistry labs. Anything that is intelligible to an intelligent layman is a way to the understanding of the world they live in and write about.

Some of that is the activity of active and curious minds, for the sake of the activity. Part has a practical usefulness.

A fiction writer, in particular, has to be a jack of all

knowledges. If his fiction involves an Episcopal wedding, he has to know or find out the Episcopal marriage service, not to mention the Episcopal state of mind. The most casual acts of his characters may touch areas outside his own immediate experience, and states of mind other than his own. So, he reads, not committing reading for the sake of the information, but picking up all sorts of information in the course of reading that is done with only curiosity and interest for its motivation.

❑ *Then, should instruction in creative writing be concerned, at least in some part, with the handling of factual matter, of information?*

Yes. There is no substitute for really knowing what you are talking about. The books with staying power are the ones that speak from large knowledge and add something to a reader's comprehension. But it is sometimes possible, and perhaps even legitimate, to fake, too.

You remember the Indian who was chasing the rabbit? He chased the rabbit because he hadn't eaten for three days. And he was very persistent; he chased the rabbit up and down and across, until he finally cornered him. Then, as he was fitting an arrow and drawing back his bow, the rabbit sat up and said, "Arf arf!" The Indian was astonished, and eased up on the bow and said: "What kind of rabbit are you? Are you really a rabbit, and are you *barking* at me?" "Oh, I'm a rabbit, all right," the rabbit said, "but in a tight place it's well to be bilingual."

In a tight place in a novel it is well to be bilingual, too. It is necessary to be able to fake. We all do it—vamp in a bass and cover up our deficiencies, with an air of confidence.

Nevertheless, there is generally no substitute for knowing what you are talking about. Many fictions, whether they involve history or some aspect of contemporary life not in the common experience, or science or small-town politics or the techniques of fighting forest fires, represent more knowledge, both from experience and from research, than shows on the surface.

This, too, is something that should be taught to a class, if only to dissipate the vulgar error that writing is easy, because it only involves "making words." Words must be *about* something, and making them isn't easy, by a long shot. It is not a frivolous pursuit. It should be taken as seriously as the search for the replicating machinery in the DNA of the *E. coli* virus X170.

Rigor is what we are talking about, a responsibility to a certain kind of truth and to observed reality. The worst writing classes with which I have had any experience have been the soft ones—the mutual admiration societies in which whatever is said, if it is said well, is right. A teacher who permits that sort of atmosphere to develop gives his students a profoundly wrong impression of the profession and of the professional's obligations.

Once or twice I have taken over a class after it had been handled for a term by a soft and indulgent teacher who gave everybody A, exacted no penalties for late work or no work, and uncritically accepted the "truth" of what was written by his students. Those teachers were good people and good writers, but they were not good teachers of writing, because they demanded too little. After one term under their direction, the class was spoiled; winter term and spring term were wasted time. Students get no benefit from that kind of indulgent teaching. Their only hope is to recover from it.

❏ *Would you speak next about the teaching of the "craft" aspects of writing, such as literary devices or techniques?*

The question of how much "craft" one should and can teach is always open, as is the question of how directly and systematically one should teach it.

It is fatal (though by no means unheard of) for a teacher to impress his own craft, as well as his own conceptions, upon his students. It is, however, common practice to send a student out to learn a particular technique by studying a particular writer who was good at it: Joyce, say, for stream of consciousness or Conrad for the tricks of multiple narrators.

But I have never found it very useful to do this in a vacuum, just as a general exercise. If a student is struggling with a story involving narrators within narrators, he obviously should know *Lord Jim*. If he wants to report experience in the undifferentiated, unaccented flow of a consciousness, he must know Joyce, Dorothy Richardson, Virginia Woolf, and some other people. Maybe they will only teach him how not to proceed, but that is something.

I believe the need should give rise to the assignment— that, actually, the merest hint, in the discussion of a manuscript, is enough to send the young writer to the places that might be instructive. Abstract rules of technique are not useful unless someone has an occasion for their use, and finds himself deficient.

I have never believed in assigning an entire writing class a certain body of reading. That will do for literature classes, where the problem is different. But a writer is a whole individual, stealing from whoever can help him, and ranging all of life and literature for his clues. Assigning him set readings would be like sending a young Dalí or Braque or Monet to copy the *Mona Lisa* or *Blue Boy*. It would be a way to make academic writers, not good ones.

Many of the best clues to craft come out of the class manuscripts under discussion. A telling phrase, an evocative paragraph, a swift clue to character, can be rolled on the tongue and rung on the table—and perhaps do more than Milton can.

❑ *Should the teacher, in the process of instruction, consciously try to shape a student's personality or to enlarge him or her as a human being?*

Well, I have some fairly strong feelings about that. I do not believe I can teach anybody how to be a bigger or better or more humane person. But I do subscribe to the notion that in order to write a great poem one should be, in some sense or other, a great poet. That suggests that any writer had better be concerned with the development of his personality and his character.

I don't believe, with Oscar Wilde, that the fact that a man is a poisoner has nothing to do with his prose. It does have something to do with his prose. A poisoner will write a poisoner's prose, however beautiful. Even if it has nothing to do with private life, personal morality, or his general ethical character, being a poisoner suggests some flaw somewhere—in the sensibility or humanity or compassion or the largeness of mind—that is going to reflect itself in the prose.

Most artists are flawed; but they probably ought to make the effort not to be. But how do you teach people to enlarge themselves in order to enlarge their writing? It is a little like asking them to "commit experience" for literary purposes.

Largeness is a lifelong matter—sometimes a conscious goal, sometimes not. You enlarge yourself because that is the kind of individual you are. You grow because you are not content *not* to. You are like a beaver that chews constantly because if it doesn't, its teeth grow long and lock. You grow because you are a grower; you're large because you can't stand to be small.

If you are a grower and a writer as well, your writing should get better and larger and wiser. But how you teach that, the Lord knows.

I guess you can suggest the *ideal* of it, the notion that it is a good thing to be large and magnanimous and wise, that it is a better aim in life than pleasure or money or fame. By comparison, it seems to me, pleasure and money, and probably fame as well, are contemptible goals.

I would go so far as to say that to a class. But not all of the class would believe me.

❑ *Have you any observations to make on adherence to a working regimen or routine, which is often cited as a discipline necessarily associated with being a writer?*

Different kinds of writers devise different strategies. My

own experience is primarily that of the novelist, and a novel is a long, long agony. When Bill Styron described it as like setting out to walk from Vladivostok to Spain on your knees, he was not just making a phrase.

You must submerge in a novel—or *I* must. It must be real to you as you work at it, and the only way I know to make it real is to dive into it at eight in the morning and not emerge until lunchtime. Then, for the space of each working day, it can be as real as the other life you live—the one from lunch to bedtime.

I know no way to become convinced, and stay convinced, of the reality and worthiness of a novel but to go out every morning to the place where writing is done, and put your seat on the seat of the chair, as Sinclair Lewis advised, and keep it there.

It is not an easy discipline for everyone. Young writers often rebel against it, because when they go off by themselves, day after day, they get restless.

It is the dullness of writing that they must invoke; they must actively seek it; they must put themselves in a prison and stare across a typewriter at a wall for four or five hours a day, seven days a week. It had better be seven, too, not six, not five—certainly not two or three.

Nocturnals may find the quiet of past-midnight a better time than morning. Poets and playwrights and short-story writers, accustomed to bursts of intense work, will not need this long concentration. But everybody will benefit from a good, deep, well-worn, and familiar rut.

It is a good test of the depth of one's commitment, actually. Nobody can make you go there except yourself, and you will make yourself go there only because that is where you want to be, that is what you must be doing.

❑ *From the teacher's personal standpoint, are there any special dangers against which he or she must be on guard?*

There are several. One is that concern about students' work will crowd out application to your own. It is fairly easy for teachers of writing to become ex-writers.

Another is that the necessarily different preoccupations and approaches of successively newer generations of writers will lead the writing teacher into a cosmetic youthfulness— into imitation of his students—and lead him to forget what his own life has taught him. It is exhilarating, but often dangerous, to give up your own hard-won ground and try to gain stamping-space on someone else's.

Finally, there is the problem of extended foster-fatherhood. Young writers may come to depend on a teacher they respect; and because they think of him as the one with experience, connections, and answers, they may continue to lean on him—perhaps for life.

Once committed to the parental role, a teacher can be swamped—in the pleasantest way possible—by old friendship and by the desire to help these young people whom he has known as beginners. Their collective need can swallow his whole life. It really can.

That is one reason I quit teaching. And even after quitting, I can't escape it. In more than forty years of teaching, I collected a lot of ex-students; and because I had the luck to be able to pick them for talent, an extraordinary number of them are publishing writers. I get to read a lot of galleys.

❑ *To what extent should the teacher try to become internal to what students write, internal to their actual creative process of writing?*

The internal part is the student's own business. Only he or she knows what is intended; only he or she can perform or realize it. A teacher should understand that intention, but not try to control it. He doesn't have to invent this young writer, he only has to help train him.

There are, of course, plenty of writing teachers who create cliques and coteries. I find them reprehensible—the wrong kind, bent on producing clones of themselves or their cult figures.

Negative capability, a phrase that Keats used, is what is needed here: sympathy, empathy, a capacity to enter into another mind without dominating it. Strong-minded teachers with narrow views of their function are more likely to give a student attitudes he must live down, than help in assuming his own full stature.

❑ *If our colleges and universities are today, as you have indicated, this country's principal centers for the teaching of creative writing, how has that circumstance come to be the case?*

Writing instruction is something that did not exist in our colleges until the 20th Century. So far as I know, the other countries where it occurs have copied it from us. In some countries it still doesn't exist.

It began with Dean Le Baron Russell Briggs of Harvard, who early in the century began teaching a class that required a daily theme. (Those were the hard old days, before rigor was relaxed.) Many, many American writers came out of Dean Briggs's class—and at least one of them, Robert Benchley, went on writing daily 800-word themes all his professional life.

Charles Townsend Copeland, also at Harvard, followed Dean Briggs's lead. Between the two, they must have trained half the American writers of their time.

Later, in the 1940s, when I was teaching at Harvard, Theodore Morrison created five positions in the writing section of the English department, called "Briggs-Copeland Faculty Instructors of English Composition," commemorating the role that Briggs and Copeland had played. By that time, of course, writing instruction had been carried to the farthest corners of the country. It was a staple, though minor, offering at the University of Utah when I was a student there in the 1920s.

The second step in a movement which has been progressive for a good many years was the founding of the Bread Loaf Writers' Conference at Bread Loaf, Vermont, one of the summer campuses of Middlebury College. That, the first of its kind so far as I know, stemmed pretty directly from Harvard—though Robert Frost and John Farrar of the publishing firm Farrar, Straus were principal founding fathers.

Farrar was the first director, but was soon succeeded by Morrison, who ran it for years, with a teaching staff drawn partly from Harvard and dominated, for those years, by Frost, Bernard DeVoto, and Louis Untermeyer. That staff gathered for two weeks at the end of every August to make academia and bohemia work in harness. They lectured, read manuscripts, conducted seminars and workshops, played a lot of tennis, drank too much.

If Bread Loaf had lasted one day longer each year, the whole mountain would have blown up. But for fourteen days, the effects were often salutary. Young writers got all the stimulus they could stand; staff gave until they were drained.

Bread Loaf became a model for many other conferences, many of them in regional centers—some in mountain resort areas, such as Aspen and Sun Valley and Squaw Valley.

A third development began in the fall of 1930 at the State University of Iowa in Iowa City, when Norman Foerster established something called the "School of Letters," including an early version of the writing program that has become the biggest and one of the best known in the country. Foerster made it possible for a graduate student in English to get an M.A. by submitting a creative thesis—stories or poems or a novel. (I was a graduate student at Iowa in that year, and I took that option. If I was not the first creative M.A. in the country, I was one of the first two or three.)

Foerster's program went so far as to offer the Ph.D. for a creative dissertation, too; but during the Depression that did not seem like a safe teaching credential, and some of us steered away from it, in favor of more orthodox degrees. Most writing programs these days offer the M.A.—or, more likely, the M.F.A.—but stop at that, believing the Ph.D. is properly a degree in literary history or literary criticism (preparation for teaching not writing, but literature).

Nevertheless, beginning with Dean Briggs's daily-theme course and coming to a climax with the Iowa program and its imitators, writing had moved into the academy in a big way. As late as the end of the Twenties, the customary way for a writer to get his apprenticeship (both in experience and in actual writing) was to begin as a newspaperman. Many did it. Sinclair Lewis, Dreiser, Hemingway—and, before them, Howells and Mark Twain and Richard Harding Davis and Stephen Crane—all wrote their way off newspapers and into books.

It is very different now. Because in America it has never been easy for writers—and especially for serious writers—to make a living by their writing alone, many have had to seek backlog jobs. The revolution that put writing into the colleges created a lot of jobs, and they were particularly desirable because they could be for only a term or two—and in every case involved a three- or four-month break in the summer.

College programs also bred a new lecture and reading circuit. The result is that nearly every American writer you can name is associated either with some academy or with the academic lecture-platform circuit.

Writers used to be somewhat contemptuous of the colleges, and college English departments used to look with some suspicion on writers, as underbred wild men. Now the relationship is Cold War at worst; more often, a cold truce; and in some happy cases, a warm collaboration. Whatever the relationship, colleges are where most of our writers can be found.

❏ *Do you favor having, as is now typically the case, creative-writing instruction centered within English departments?*

As I have said, the relationship isn't always smooth. English departments have, with some grumbling, made room for writers, feeling (sometimes with justification) that these people can sling words but are lacking in both learning and culture. The writers, on the other hand, often take the view that English teachers are disappointed writers, that they teach because they can't *do,* and that envy and jealousy are behind their resistance to the full academic acceptance of writers.

I think that, with time, those prejudices wear away. Poetry and fiction are normally accepted as publications that warrant the promotion of their authors, and there are some English departments whose principal claim to distinction is their writing section.

One thing should be said. No matter how warmly an English department welcomes a writing program, it should not have full control of it, especially of the selection of its writing teachers.

English departments are notorious breeding places for cliques and coteries. Their professors, if they are not mainly trained in the same graduate schools, are trained in the same system, and by scholars who are not infrequently systems-makers. Their training, moreover, is in reading, criticism, literary history—not in writing.

When they are allowed to pick writing teachers, they often pick what I feel are the wrong kind: esoterics, cult figures, bearers of some advanced or arcane True Faith.

I believe that the catholicity of a writing program, and the flexibility of its teaching, is better served by writers picked by their fellow writers.

❑ *Has our literature been influenced, in any particular manner or to any appreciable extent, by the fact that the teaching of creative writing has, here in America, been so preponderantly centered within colleges and universities?*

That is hard to say. The writing that goes on in colleges and universities, both by students and by teachers, is likely to be as free from commercial pressures as writing anywhere. And that is both a safety and a danger, for whatever one may say about commercial pressures, they do squeeze out some of the lunatic fringe.

A coterie within an English department does just the opposite—encourages the experimental (and, sometimes, lunatic), with the assumption that it is "purer" than the writing that has publication as its goal. English departments' writing programs are not always hermetic, but there is that danger.

I doubt that the fads which sweep English departments—everything from the New Humanism to Reductionism—have much effect on the actual writing of the country, which is incorrigibly closer to life than the fads are.

But it is possible that a discerning critic might find in the literature of the last four or five decades—the period during which writing has established itself in our schools—a greater tendency to split hairs, a somewhat greater openness to the formation of "schools" (in the European sense), and a somewhat greater willingness to "experiment"—experiment being generally imitation of Joyce, who otherwise has not had an enormous influence on the art of fiction in America.

❑ *How, precisely, would one go about actually setting up a program in creative writing?*

I had to grapple with that problem when I moved from Harvard to Stanford, at the end of World War II. Suddenly, I was surrounded by G.I. students just out of the armed services, much more mature than the ordinary college student, with many more things to write, and with a sense of urgency brought on by three or four years of lost time in the army or navy.

What could I do, in a provincial university, three thousand miles from New York and an hour from San Francisco, that would help and encourage these obviously gifted people? I had the experience of Harvard, Iowa, and the Bread Loaf Writers' Conference, as well as the example of the Hopwood Awards at the University of Michigan, to guide me; and I borrowed from them all.

First of all, I wanted fellowship money, to buy some time for these writers. That has been the function of Guggenheim and other fellowship programs, and it needs no further justification.

Next, on the model of the Hopwood Awards, I thought we needed prizes; and we set them up. Later we abandoned them, because they bred a too-virulent spirit of competition, and because the problem of finding able and distinguished judges became too difficult.

Next, we needed money for some visitors, writers of distinction who could be brought to the campus for a day or a week or a term. Over the years we brought Robert Frost, Katherine Anne Porter, Elizabeth Bowen, Hortense Calisher, Walter Van Tilburg Clark, Frank O'Connor, Malcolm Cowley, and many more—some of them several times. They added immensely to the program. Like the fellowships, they turned out to be essential.

What else did we use our money for? Beyond fellowships, visitors, and the soon-abandoned prizes, nothing much—a little aid in publication, to put into book form the stories and poems produced by the annual crop of young writers.

The rest of the program was pretty standard English-department routines: a ladder of courses, from beginner to graduate, all taught by writers; and the privilege of submitting a group of stories or poems or a novel, as an M.A. thesis.

If you have gifted students—and we have never lacked them at Stanford—that is about all you need.

❑ *That leads to the consideration of what really does happen within the classroom of a creative-writing program?*

Certainly one function of a writing class is to lift students out of classroom amateurism and bring them into contact with professional aims and attitudes, either in the person of the teacher or of a visiting writer or of the members of the class themselves—or, sometimes, in books. The best possible justification for a writing class is that it should make students competent to deal with the word in all its manifestations.

As Robert Frost used to say, people have to know how far to trust a metaphor. Trust it too far, and it can break under you—and teach you the perils of analogy. That and many other things are best learned in the laboratory of pen, paper, and wastebasket; and in a writing class all the members are utilizing that lab simultaneously.

Another thing you may learn in a writing class is the ability to take and profit from criticism. How do you react when your cherished eloquence falls on deaf ears? At the very least, you should make a note that there are different kinds of ears and that what seems obvious or eloquent to you is dull or common to another sensibility.

I have had students who could neither give nor take criticism, without getting fiery red in the face and rough in the voice—so sensitive to personal slight that they could neither take it themselves nor dish it out, without a heavy component of hostility. Untreated, that disease can be fatal; even treated, it is uncomfortable.

If criticism affects you that way, you are very unlikely to "make it" as a writer, because there is no way to learn, except through criticism—your own or someone else's.

A writing seminar exerts criticism ad hoc upon a specific manuscript. A member of the class provides the subject matter, the class the discussion, the teacher no more than a mild Socratic guidance. Instead of a lecture, what goes on is a discussion which, with luck, may lead to some sort of illumination or consensus.

It is very difficult to do, actually. After two hours of apparently mild semi-participation, the teacher can come out feeling as if he had carried a piano up the stairs.

Sometimes, too—and this happens even to some of the most talented students—the class has a tendency to think of writing as spasmodic activity, and the class likewise. They are young people, full of hormones and themselves and other concerns, and they like a good time as well as the next person. Moreover, unless they are special students, taking only writing, they have plenty of other work to do.

It is, therefore, sometimes hard to keep enough copy coming in to keep the class—especially if it is a small class—running. If there is no copy, we might just as well adjourn. That generally shames a class into getting busy, and helps develop the working habit that is probably the most important habit any writer needs to have. He has to learn it for himself, but a class that acts as a deadline—a hard deadline—can help him do it.

What else? A teacher can quietly squelch public confession (which is tempting to some writers) and public exhibitionism (which is just as tempting). The class itself is likely to do it for him. After all, if you "spill your guts" on the floor, you have to expect people to step on them—and that can be educational; it can teach you either not to spill your guts or to follow Frost's advice, and spill them as if they belonged to someone else.

By and large, a good writing class functions like a form of publication. Abruptly, this manuscript—this thing that was a scribbled page—is put into a posture of dignity, demanding attention. A tableful of people have listened to it; you yourself have listened to it, have heard yourself read it. It has been tested by both eye and ear, and is being tried now by this group whose opinions you may not always agree with, but have to attend to.

Merely having a story read aloud and discussed makes it, in its author's eyes, more serious and more worthy. And that group around the table may be the best audience, though not the biggest, that that writer will have in his life.

Publication itself, of course, carries the process much further. No piece of writing is fully real until it is published. Merely seeing it in a typeface that is not a typewriter face will do it. *This* was actually set up by a printer and run through a press. Marvelous! And *I* did it. Suddenly, it is three times as important as when it was only a typescript.

Every writer who "makes it" at all has that experience. But it may be a long time coming. Publication through a reading in class is the next-best thing—and far more immediate. It will probably happen several times to each member of a class during the term, and it will ultimately separate the men from the boys.

The essentials are only two: taking a piece of writing seriously; and criticizing it with a view to helping it be what it wants to be. It cannot be done without some degree of abrasion. You don't sharpen a knife on a cake of soap.

❑ *You have said it is the teacher's task to "manage the environment" of a writing class. Would you speak now about how that is achieved?*

Managing the environment for a group of talented (and frequently headstrong) people is not easy. I have often thought of it as comparable to the way one trains a hot-blooded colt, whose whole impulse is to run. You put him in a corral and you let him run—in circles, with a rope on him. You don't yank his head off, and you don't let him run over you. You teach him to run under control. And much of his control is going to be learned from the other horses in the corral.

A writing class is inevitably competitive, do you see? Everyone's primary concern is his own success, and that success, when something as personal as literature is involved, is acutely personal. But if you encourage competition, or let it run rampant, any individual's success becomes everyone else's envy.

Ideally, if the class mix and the teacher's wisdom operate right, every individual's success becomes everyone else's stimulation. The people in such a class, if it is well selected, are roughly equal in talent and opportunity. If one puts a story in *The New Yorker* or gets an enthusiastic acceptance of his novel, other members of the class have a right to feel that the possibility is all the more available to them.

That successful one is no better than I am, they will think. The gift there is different from mine, but not superior. What happened to him is bound, sooner or later, if I work, to happen to me.

For some such reason, in seminars that jelled properly, I have seen people write better than they will ever write again—write better than they really know how to. The trick is to keep the competitiveness friendly, to see to it that individual success stimulates other members of the group, instead of depressing and discouraging them.

❑ *What about the creative-writing teacher's concerns centering upon grammar and syntax and the like?*

There are two kinds of teaching at issue here. One of them is the plain instruction—often the corrective instruction—in the communication of meaning through language. That goes on in "Freshman English" classes and in the kind of exposition courses often offered to engineers and other professional trainees.

It is absolutely essential—the white man's burden—and it is never done well enough. It has its basis in grammar and syntax, which are simply the logic of the language. (No two languages have quite the same logic, but each within itself is consistent.)

Inevitably, that kind of teaching has a certain place in a creative-writing course. I take it as a basic principle that anyone who aspires to use his native tongue professionally and publicly had better know it. I have spent a lot of time going over manuscripts with students, in the way an editor might go over them, to clean them up and make them presentable, and keep the author from appearing in public with his shirt-tail out and egg on his tie.

That is not the truly important matter, but it is one of the things that can be taught, and it is not trivial—though young writers, full of fire and the will to unbridled originality, sometimes think it is.

Grammar and syntax are more important in fiction than in poetry, which can proceed by daring leaps. When a fiction writer dissolves grammar, syntax, and logic, he is in grave danger of dissolving everything he is trying to communicate. If he cannot be restrained or directed, he must be permitted to go his way, but he had better know what he is risking. If he tells me, "Don't try to figure it out, just groove on it," I am at least going to make it difficult for him to get away with it, without an argument.

So, whether dismembered syntax has sprung from ignorance or from the lust after originality, I believe it should be questioned. After all, all a reader knows is the marks on the printed page. Those marks have to contribute meaning— every meaning the story or poem is going to have.

We are dealing with a complicated symbolic system, and every element of that system, down to the conventional signs for pauses and nuances, has had a long testing. Its function is to help reproduce in cold print what was a human voice speaking for human ears. The system can be challenged— and, even, cracked—but it is challenged at the writer's peril, and he had better know it before he undertakes to change it. A good writing class can help him discover what works and what does not.

❑ *A final question, Mr. Stegner: Beyond developing a student's technical proficiencies and the influencing of his or her literary awareness, sensitivity, and understanding, can the teacher of creative writing actually induce or evoke talent—really cause talent to come into being?*

A teacher probably can't, but a class sometimes can. No, let me qualify that. Talent can't be taught, but it can be awakened—by reading, by contact with other talents, by exposure to an environment where the expression of talent is valued and encouraged. And once it is awakened, it can be guided—unless it happens to be too headstrong, as it sometimes is. (If it is absolutely headstrong, it must be allowed to go its own hard way.)

I cannot say often enough that the teaching of writing is Socratic. The end is not the production of clones of any approved style or writer—and certainly not of the teacher! The end is the full development of what is unique in the young writer, without encouraging him in mere eccentricity.

Writing is a social act, an act of communication both intellectual and emotional. It is also, at its best, an act of affirmation—a way of joining the human race and a human culture. And that means a writer must have a clear conception not only of the self, but of the society.

After all, the language itself is an inheritance, a shared wealth. It may be played with, stretched, forced, bent; but I, as a writer or teacher, must never assume that it is mine. It is *ours*, the living core, as well as the instrument, of the culture I derive from, resist, challenge, and—ultimately—serve.

But, no, nobody can teach anyone else to have a talent. All a teacher can do is set high goals for students—or get them to set them for themselves—and, then, try to help them reach those goals.

A college class seems to me one of the best places for that sort of guidance.

TO A
YOUNG WRITER

YOUR NOTE ASKS ADVICE on some purely practical matters, and to most of your questions the answers are dead-easy. No, you don't need any agent yet; later you probably will. Yes, you might try lifting sections out of your book and trying them on magazines; it can do no harm, and it might get you an audience or make you some money or both. No, there is no reason why you shouldn't apply for one of the available fellowships: Guggenheim or Saxton or, since you are uncommitted, one of those offered by publishers. By the same token, you are eligible to submit your book to any prize contest and to apply for admission to any of the literary and artistic colonies, such as Yaddo, the MacDowell Colony, or the Huntington Hartford Foundation. Even a brief residence in one of these would give you a place to live and write and would remove at least for a few weeks or months the insecurity that has nearly unnerved you. Of course I will write letters to any of these places in your behalf, of course I will give you letters to publishers, and if we happen to be in New York at the same time I will be happy to take you up to an office or two or three and introduce you.

But when I have said this, I am left feeling that most of

what you really hoped to hear has been left unsaid. I suspect that much of the reason for your writing me was a need for reassurance: Your confidence had suddenly got gooseflesh and damp palms; you came up out of your book and looked around you and were hit by sudden panic. You would like to be told that you are good and that all this difficulty and struggle and frustration will give way gradually or suddenly, preferably suddenly, to security, fame, confidence, the conviction of having worked well and faithfully to a good end and become someone important to the world. If I am wrong in writing to this unspoken plea, forgive me; it is the sort of thing I felt myself at your age, and still feel, and will never get over feeling.

It is no trouble to tell you that you indeed are good, much too good to remain unpublished. Because publishers are mainly literate and intelligent, most of them are sure to see the quality in your novel, and one of them is sure to publish it. But that is as far as I can honestly go in reassurance, for I suspect he will publish it with little expectation of its making much money, either for him or for you.

Naturally I am not saying anything as foolish as that literary worth and popularity are incompatible. They are proved compatible quite frequently, but almost always when the writer in question possesses some form of the common touch—humor, sentiment, violence, sensationalism, sex, a capacity for alarm—and raises it to the level of art. Shakespeare and Rabelais and Mark Twain didn't exhaust the possibilities of lifting a whole mass of common preoccupations into beauty and significance. But it is your misfortune (and also your specific virtue) to have an uncommon touch. Your virtues are not the virtues of the mass of the population, or even of the reading population. Restraint, repose, compassion, humor that isn't ribald and feeling that isn't sentimental—these are caviar to the general, whatever you and I might wish.

You write better than hundreds of people with established literary reputations. You understand your characters and their implications, and you take the trouble to make sure that they have implications. Without cheating or bellowing or tearing a passion to tatters, you can bring a reader to that alert participation that is the truest proof of fiction's effectiveness. You think ten times where a lot of writers throb once.

And there is very little demand for the cool, perfect things you can do. You have gone threadbare for ten years to discover that your talents are almost sure to go unappreciated.

It is one thing to go threadbare for five or ten years in show business or to spend eight or ten years on a medical or legal education. A man can do it cheerfully, for the jackpots are there in those professions and may be expected by the talented in the course of time. And I suspect that you have had somewhere before you the marshlight of a jackpot, too. After all, every publishing season produces that happy sound of someone's apron being filled with solid, countable money. Your own seven years in college and two and a half years of apprenticeship on this first novel should entitle you to at least the milder sorts of expectation.

Since I participated in it, I know something about your education, and I know that it took. A literary education does not necessarily turn out even a good reader, much less a good writer. But with you it did both. You are a sharpened instrument, ready and willing to be put to work.

For one thing, you never took writing to mean self-expression, which means self-indulgence. You understood from the beginning that writing is done with words and sentences, and you spent hundreds of hours educating your ear, writing and rewriting and rewriting until you began to handle words in combination as naturally as one changes tones with the tongue and lips in whistling. I speak respectfully of this part of your education, because every year I see students who will not submit to it—who have only themselves to say and who are bent upon saying it without concessions to the English language. In acknowledging that the English language is a difficult instrument and that a person who sets out to use it expertly has no alternative but to learn it, you did something else. You forced yourself away from that obsession with self that is the strength of a very few writers and the weakness of so many. You have labored to put yourself in charge of your material; you have not fallen for the romantic fallacy that it is virtue to be driven by it. By submitting to language, you submitted to other disciplines, you learned distance and detachment, you learned how to avoid muddying a story with yourself.

That much the study of writing in college has given you. It might have given you worse things as well, but didn't. It might have made you a coterie writer, might have imprinted on you some borrowed style or some arrogance of literary snobbery, might have made you forever a leaner and a dependent. How many times have I backpedaled from some young man furious to destroy with words the father he thinks he hates; how many times have I turned cold to avoid becoming a surrogate father or even mother. How much compulsive writing have I read, inwardly flinching for the helpless enslavement it revealed. How often the writing of young writers is a way of asserting a personality that isn't yet there, that is only being ravenously hunted for.

None of that in yours. In yours, sanity and light and compassion, not self-love and self-pity. You know who you are, and you are good. Never doubt it—though you could not be blamed if you wistfully wondered. To date, from all your writing, you have made perhaps five hundred dollars, for two short stories and a travel article. To finance school and to write your novel you have lived meagerly with little encouragement and have risked the disapproval of your family, who have understandably said, "Here is this girl nearly thirty years old now, unmarried, without a job or a profession, still mooning away at her writing as if life were forever. Here goes her life through her fingers while she sits in cold rooms and grows stoop-shouldered over a typewriter." So now, with your book finally in hand, you want desperately to have some harvest: a few good reviews, some critical attention, encouragement, royalties enough to let you live and go on writing.

You are entitled to them all, but you may get few or none of them. Some good reviews you undoubtedly will get, but also many routine plus-minus ones that will destroy you with their impercipience, and a few flip ones by bright young men who will patronize you in five hundred words or spend their space telling how trying was the heat on the New Haven as they read this book on the commuters' special. Your initial royalty statement, at an optimistic guess, will indicate that your publisher by hard work built up an advance sale of 2,700 copies. Your next one, six months later, will probably carry the news that 432 of those copies came back and that altogether you fell just a little short of earning the thousand-dollar advance that you spent eight or nine months ago.

All this you are aware of as possibility, because you have the habit of not deceiving yourself and because you have seen it happen to friends. Learn to look upon it as probability.

Having brought yourself to that glum anticipation, ponder your choices. To go on writing as you have been do-ing—slowly, carefully, with long pauses for thinking and revising—you need some sort of subsidy: fellowship, ad-vance, grant, job, marriage, something. In the nature of things, most of your alternatives will be both temporary and modest. Of the possible jobs, teaching probably offers most, because its hours are flexible and because it entails a three-month summer vacation. You have the training, the degrees, some teaching experience, but for you I would not advise teaching. For one thing, you are so conscientious that you would let it absorb your whole energy. For another, I am sure you can write only if you have full time for it. Your distilla-tion process is slow, drop by drop, and you can't make it pro-duce enough in a few broken weeks of summer. So you will undoubtedly try the fellowships and the colonies, and per-haps for a year or two get by that way.

After that, who knows? You might sell enough to squeak by; you might get a job caring for people's cats while they travel; you might work for a year or two at a time and save enough to take every third year for writing; you might marry. You might even marry and keep on writing, though it often happens otherwise. By the same token, you might find that marriage and children are so adequate a satisfaction of the urges that are driving you to write that you don't need to write, or you may find all the satisfactions of marriage and a family and come back to fiction when your children are grown. You and I both know those who have, and we both know some of the special difficulties they met. However you do it, I imagine you will always be pinched—for money, for time, for a place to work. But I think you will do it. And believe me, it is not a new problem. You are in good company.

Barring marriage, which is an alternative career and not a solution of this one, you may say to yourself that you can't stand such a narrow, gray life, that you will modify your temperament and your taste, and work into your books some of the sensationalism, violence, shock, sentiment, sex, or Great Issues that you think may make them attractive to a large audience. I doubt that you could do it if you wanted to, and I am certain that you shouldn't try, for you cannot write with a whole heart things that are contrary to your nature. The fine things in your first novel are there because you wrote them with a whole heart, from an intense conviction. Trying to write like those who manage a large popular success, you may succeed, because you have brains and skill; but however proper success may be for others, in you, and on these terms, it will not be legitimate, for you will have stopped being the writer that you respected.

You are as whole an instrument as a broom. The brush is no good without the handle, and the whole thing is good only for sweeping. You are scheduled—doomed—to be a serious writer regarding life seriously and reporting it to a small audience. Other kinds of writers are both possible and necessary, but this is the kind you are, and it is a good kind. Not many of your countrymen will read you or know your name, not because they are Americans, or moderns, or especially stupid, but because they are human. Your kind of writer has never spoken to a large audience except over a long stretch of time, and I would not advise you to pin too much hope even on posterity. Your touch is the uncommon touch; you will speak only to the thoughtful reader. And more times than once you will ask yourself whether such readers really exist at all and why you should go on projecting your words into silence like an old crazy actor playing the part of himself to an empty theater.

The readers do exist. Jacques Barzun confidently guesses that there are at least thirty thousand of them in the United States, though they may have to be found vertically through many years rather than horizontally in any one publishing season, and though the hope of your reaching them all is about like the possibility of your tracking down all the surviving elk in America. But any of them you find you will treasure. This audience, by and large, will listen to what you say and not demand that you say what everyone else is saying or what some fashionable school or clique says you should say. They are there, scattered through the apparently empty

theater, listening and making very little noise. Be grateful for
them. But however grateful you are, never, never write to
please them.

The moment you start consciously writing for an audience, you begin wondering if you are saying what the
audience wants or expects. The peculiar virtue of this audience is that it leaves up to you what should be said. You have
heard Frank O'Connor speak of the difference between the
private and the public arts. Unless it is being dramatized or
read aloud over the radio, fiction is one of the private ones.
The audience has nothing to do with its making or with the
slant it takes. You don't discover what should go into your
novel by taking a poll or having a trial run in Boston or
Philadelphia. You discover it by thinking and feeling your
way into a situation or having it feel its way into you. From
inside a web of relationships, from the very heart of a temperament, your imagination creates outward and forward.

You write to satisfy yourself and the inevitabilities of the
situation you have started in motion. You write under a compulsion, it is true, but it is the compulsion of your situation,
not of a private hatred or envy or fear; and you write to satisfy yourself, but you write always in the remote awareness of
a listener—O'Connor's man in the armchair. He responds to
what you respond to and understands what you understand.
Above all, he listens. Being outside of you, he closes a circuit,
he is an ear to your mouth. Unless at least one like him reads
you, you have written uselessly. Your book is as hypothetical
as the sound of the tree that falls in the earless forest.

Nevertheless, I repeat, except for vaguely imagining him
and hoping he is there, ignore him, do not write what you

think he would like. Write what *you* like. When your book is published, you will have a letter from at least one of him, perhaps from as many as twenty or thirty of him. With luck, as other books come on his numbers will grow. But to you he will always be a solitary reader, an ear, not an audience. Literature speaks to temperament, Conrad says. Your books will find the temperaments they can speak to.

And I would not blame you if you still asked, Why bother to make contact with kindred spirits you never see and may never hear from, who perhaps do not even exist except in your hopes? Why spend ten years in an apprenticeship to fiction only to discover that this society so little values what you do that it won't pay you a living wage for it?

Well, what goes on in your novel—the affectionate revelation of a relationship, the unraveling of the threads of love and interest binding a family together, the tranquil and not so tranquil emotions surrounding the death of a beloved and distinguished grandfather—this is closer to what happens in church than to what happens in the theater. Fiction always moves toward one or another of its poles, toward drama at one end or philosophy at the other. This book of yours is less entertainment than philosophical meditation presented in terms of personalities in action. It is serious, even sad; its colors and lights are autumnal. You have not loved Chekhov for nothing—maybe you imagined him as your reader in the armchair. He would listen while you told him the apparently simple thing you want to say: how love lasts, but changes, how life is full of heats and frustrations, causes and triumphs, and death is cool and quiet. It does not sound like much, summarized, and yet it embodies everything you believe about yourself and about human life and at least some aspects of the people you have most loved. In your novel, anguish and resignation are almost in balance. Your people live on the page and in the memory, because they have been loved and therefore have been richly imagined.

Your book is dramatized belief; and because in everyday life we make few contacts as intimate as this with another temperament and another mind, these scenes have an effect of cool shock—first almost embarrassment, then acknowledgment. Yes, I want to say. Yes, this is how it would be.

I like the sense of intimate knowing that your novel gives me. After all, what are any of us after but the conviction of belonging? What does more to stay us and keep our backbones stiff while the world reels than the sense that we are linked with someone who listens and understands and so in some way completes us? I have said somewhere else that the aesthetic experience is a conjugal act, like love. I profoundly believe it.

The worst thing that could happen to the ferocious seekers after identity is that they should find it and it only. There are many who do their best to escape it. Of our incorrigible and profound revulsion against identity, I suppose that physical love is the simplest, most immediate, and for many the only expression. Some have their comfort in feeling that they belong to the world of nature, big brother to the animals and cousin to the trees; some commit themselves to the kingdom of God. There is much in all of them, but for you, I imagine, not enough in any. For you it will have to be the kingdom of man, it will have to be art. You have nothing to gain and nothing to give except as you distill and purify ephemeral experience into quiet, searching, touching little stories like the one you have just finished, and so give your uncommon readers a chance to join you in the solidarity of pain and love and the vision of human possibility.

But isn't it enough? For lack of the full heart's desire, won't it serve?

GOOD-BYE
TO ALL T——T!

NOT EVERYONE WHO LAMENTS what contemporary novelists have done to the sex act objects to the act itself, or to its mention. Some want it valued higher than fiction seems to value it; they want the word "climax" to retain some of its literary meaning. Likewise, not everyone who has come to doubt the contemporary freedom of language objects to strong language in itself. Some of us object precisely because we value it.

I acknowledge that I have used four-letter words familiarly all my life, and have put them into books with some sense that I was insisting on the proper freedom of the artist. I have applauded the extinction of those d——d emasculations of the genteel tradition and the intrusion into serious fiction of honest words with honest meanings and emphasis. I have wished, with D. H. Lawrence, for the courage to say shit before a lady, and have sometimes had my wish.

Words are not obscene: Naming things is a legitimate verbal act. And "frank" does not mean "vulgar," any more than "improper" means "dirty." What vulgar does mean is "common"; what improper means is "unsuitable." Under the right circumstances, any word is proper. But when any sort of

word, especially a word hitherto taboo and therefore notice-
able, is scattered across a page like chocolate chips through a
Toll House cookie, a real impropriety occurs. The sin is not
the use of an "obscene" word; it is the use of a loaded word
in the wrong place or in the wrong quantity. It is the sin of
false emphasis, which is not a moral but a literary lapse related to sentimentality. It is the sin of advertisers who so
plaster a highway with neon signs that you can't find the bar
or liquor store you're looking for. Like any excess, it quickly
becomes comic.

If I habitually say shit before a lady, what do I say before
a flat tire at the rush hour in Times Square or on the San
Francisco Bay Bridge? What do I say before a revelation of
the inequity of the universe? And what if the lady takes the
bit in her teeth and says shit before me?

I have been a teacher of writing for many years and have
watched this problem since it was no bigger than a man's
hand. It used to be that, with some Howellsian notion of the
young-girl audience, one tried to protect tender female members of a mixed class from the coarse language of males trying to show off. Some years ago Frank O'Connor and I agreed
on a system. Since we had no intention whatever of restrict-
ing students' choice of subject or language, and no desire to
expurgate or bowdlerize while reading their stuff aloud for
discussion, but at the same time had to deal with these young
girls of an age our daughters might have been, we an-
nounced that any stuff so strong that it would embarrass us
to read it aloud could be read by its own author.

It was no deterrent at all, but an invitation, and not only
to coarse males. For clinical sexual observation, for full ac-

ceptance of the natural functions, for discrimination in the selection of graffiti, for boldness in the use of words that it should take courage to say before a lady, give me a sophomore girl every time. Her strength is as the strength of ten, for she assumes that if one shocker out of her pretty mouth is piquant, fifty will be literature. And so do a lot of her literary idols.

Some acts, like some words, were never meant to be casual. That is why houses contain bedrooms and bathrooms. Profanity and so-called obscenities are literary resources, verbal ways of rendering strong emotion. They are not meant to occur every ten seconds, any more than—Norman Mailer to the contrary notwithstanding—orgasms are.

So I am not going to say shit before any more ladies. I am going to hunt words that have not lost their sting, and it may be I shall have to go back to gentility to find them. Pleasant though it is to know that finally a writer can make use of any word that fits his occasion, I am going to investigate the possibilities latent in restraint.

I remember my uncle, a farmer who had used four-letter words ten to the sentence ever since he learned to talk. One day he came too near the circular saw and cut half his fingers off. While we stared in horror, he stood watching the bright arterial blood pump from his ruined hand. Then he spoke, and he did not speak loud. "Aw, the dickens," he said.

I think he understood, better than some sophomore girls and better than some novelists, the nature of emphasis.

THE WRITER'S
AUDIENCE

THE MAN WHO PUBLISHES A BOOK is a man with a sending set but no receiver, broadcasting messages into space without ever knowing whether they have reached any ears. He writes his name and corks it into a bottle that he sets afloat on the ocean in the hope that some pen pal, somewhere, on whatever unpredictable coast, will find it. He drops his feather into the Grand Canyon and stands expectantly, waiting for the crash.

This is not a complaint about public neglect. It is an acknowledgment that the writing of books is a private, not a public, art. As a man from Napa wrote me recently, half-apologizing for his intrusion, "This is the only time that I have written to thank an author, but it seemed to me that in some ways an author must lead a lonely life, separated from his readers and never quite knowing if they have understood his ideas or seen his vision."

Exactly. An orator, by contrast, knows at once whether or not he is making contact. His audience is before him, he can see the whites of their eyes and hear their laughter or their murmurs or their heckling shouts, he can watch the expression on their faces and by visible symptoms tell whether he is doing ill or well, or simply not doing anything. A musician, an actor, a poet reading aloud, can do the same, for all of them are practicing public arts. Even for painters and sculptors there is a certain quality of *performance* in the way they meet their public, since a graphic artist is most often presented through gallery shows or in his own studio, and he can literally watch his work make an impact on its viewers. A composer hearing his works performed can do the same.

But a novelist or historian is rarely privileged to watch the faces of his readers as they read. Reading is private, even solitary, as a rule. Though there may still be families who keep up the pleasant habit of reading aloud, the novelist himself is not there. Though sometimes a novelist is a performer too, like Dickens or Mark Twain, and reads his stuff from the platform, that is another thing. The art of fiction has slipped over an edge and become what it is in its most primitive forms—the art of oral storytelling: a public art, a performance.

Perhaps the only place where written fiction has something like a public performance is in creative-writing workshops such as those at Stanford and other universities and colleges, where a writer reads his stuff to his fellows in the precise hope of getting the audience reaction without which he can only guess how he is doing. But this is a special situation and artificial. Once he leaves the workshop he is not likely in all his life to have as immediate, uncluttered, and for that matter intelligent a response. The rest of his life he is going to walk up and down the rims, dropping his feathers and listening.

The natural audience of the novelist is not a crowd, but

single individuals in armchairs, and they are absolutely face-
less, they can't be safely imagined or predicted—if they
could there would be a great deal more pressure by publishers upon authors to satisfy the definable wants of these
definable readers. As it is, only the most general sorts of cat-
egorization can be made. It is clear that readers tend to strat-
ify themselves according to the intellectual content of the
books they read. It is clear that more readers are women than
men. At certain times, during the flood tide of some literary
fashion, some crisis, or some social problem, readers of all
classes will gather like ions on some literarily charged pole,
as for instance in the 1960s books on John F. Kennedy and
books on race relations had an automatic acceptance.

But if your book doesn't happen to be about John F.
Kennedy or about race relations, then what? For that matter,
even if it is, you haven't any clear idea who is reading you.
Your book might be in the handbag of some old dame off on
a free airplane ride to gamble in Las Vegas, it might lie on
the dressing table of a movie actress looking for a part, it
might be read by a student writing a term paper, by a house-
wife procrastinating the breakfast dishes, by a commuter on
the New Haven or the SP, by a clergyman hunting evidence
of contemporary demoralization, by a clergyman's wife hunting vicarious thrills. God knows who reads you, unless someone happens to like or dislike your book enough to write you
a letter.

I want to remind you of some of the special characteristics of written literature, which is like no other art, not even
like music, in the distance between creator and audience. For

one thing, it makes use of language as its instrument, and language is the subtlest of all human inventions. Literature is, in the jargon of the behavioral scientists, "language-bound." Its audience is limited automatically to the literate in that tongue. This means, of course, that it is also to a degree class-bound in many societies where literacy is not universal; space-bound, languages being geographically concentrated; and time-bound, since languages die. Literature tends to stop at the borders of its civilization, and to fade with that civilization's death; and though translation does something both to extend it geographically and preserve it through time, translation preserves only a ghost or simulacrum, not the real article. Robert Frost defined poetry as what is lost in translation.

Related to the medium of language is the symbolic system by which we write it—the most difficult symbolic system utilized in any art with the possible exception of musical notation. By contrast, architecture and the graphic arts not only transcend time and space, but they operate with an intense direction; the bulls painted by Cro-Magnon priests on the walls and ceilings of the cave of Lascaux are as thrilling an experience as if they had been painted yesterday, though they are in fact perhaps 25,000 years old, older than any language we know, or any historic civilization. To duplicate in language the intense power and movement of those bulls would be difficult enough at any time, a subtler and more indirect artistic *making* than to render the muscles and poised horns and lean flanks of the bulls in paint. It involves layers of substitutes, the sound "bull" for the actual thing, the written symbols b-u-l-l for the word, a whole complex of agreed-upon responses. The programming is much more complex, and it does not last as well.

Third, written literature is like the plastic arts (and unlike the performing arts, which exist not in space but in time) in that it is subject to indefinite amounts of checking. One can turn back and refresh the memory, correct a false impression, link consequence to cause—and this means that the written story must be meticulously made, where an oral story might survive many structural flaws.

Finally, in written literature the creator benefits by none of the excitement of audience participation. This artistic meeting between artists and audience does not take place in the open, but behind closed doors—I have already said that it is no meeting at all. No choral responses aid it; it gets no benefit from repetitions and other mnemonic forms of emphasis or hypnosis. Where an appreciative crowd may move an actor or orator to outdo himself, a writer has to create the very air currents he rises on. A public-art audience often, like a mob, swings all one way, and swings the creator with it to some extent; the audience for a novel, or for any book, only infrequently can make its enthusiasm felt by the novelist, and then only indirectly and after the fact.

Obviously a writer would *like* to know whom he is talking to, and sometimes he makes an effort to talk to some particular segment of the reading public. In spite of its painful stereotypes and standardizations, America remains a wildly pluralistic society. It is made up of a hundred "special cultures" based sometimes on geography, sometimes on ethnic origin, sometimes on education or fashion or exposure to foreign influences. And so it is possible that Beats may write for Beats, sexual-revolutionists can write for sexual-revolutionists, Louis Adamic could write for Yugoslavs, historians can write for special and dedicated audiences of Civil War buffs, or frontier buffs, Mormons can write for and about Mormons, Jews for and about Jews, urban intellectuals for and about urban intellectuals. But generally speaking, none of these is an adequate audience, some of them are buried; and even if the special audience is reached, the writer has hardly any way of telling whether he reaches anybody *else*.

I can give you an example of how confused a writer may become about his audience. The late Flannery O'Connor some years ago wrote an article defending her use of the grotesque. Her justification was that people were so spiritually sluggish that you had to jar them; she distorted characters and incidents for exactly the same reason she would shout at a deaf man. And yet I never knew one of the spiritually sluggish who *read* Flannery O'Connor. The people I know who read her are spiritually pretty alert, maybe as alert as she was herself. They read her not to get a normally loud message through inadequate ears, but to rattle and titillate their normal ears by an *extra*-loud message. So it looks as if Miss O'Connor thought she was writing for an altogether different crowd of people than she actually wrote for.

The mediators between writers and readers, the people who explicate and select and judge, recommend or squelch, are of course the reviewers and critics, but though a healthy criticism is absolutely essential to healthy creation, the critics don't always live up to their full obligation. My mild com-

plaint about them is not simply an echo of the perennial
warfare between novelists and critics. Let me state my posi-
tion. I share Chekhov's feeling that a novelist seldom learns
anything from a critic and that critics are the flies that keep
the horse from plowing. Some critics seem to me to earn
Hemingway's definition as the lice that crawl on the body of
literature. Nevertheless, in the total literary ecology they
have a function, and one would feel less like calling the pest
control man and having them sprayed if they really performed that function. The difficulty is that (with certain no-
table and noble exceptions such as Malcolm Cowley and
Edmund Wilson) they tend to run in pack. They capture certain journals, literally corner the critical market the way Jay
Gould cornered the gold market, so that for ten years at a
time a single critical attitude rules, and a limited range of
books is praised, a special vocabulary springs up, bright graduate students catch the tone and the lingo and write (and
here is a case of writing with an eye very definitely on an audience) to please the reigning critics rather than to discuss a
new book in its own proper terms. For a young critic in New
York in 1964 the man in the armchair may well turn out to
be Norman Podhoretz or Lionel Trilling or Alfred Kazin, just
as a few years back he might have been Allen Tate or John
Crowe Ransom.

   To this one could not object at all if there were at all
times adequate provision for dissenting critical voices. Being
so pluralist a nation, we ought to have pluralist literature and
pluralist literary criticism. The fact is that in nothing so
much as our literary criticism do the forces of fashion and
stereotype take over. In spite of (or is it because of?) the fact

that the present reigning critics are ostentatiously poly-mathic and affect a world-tone, we have been getting essentially one kind of literature, one kind of moral and aesthetic stance, or else one kind of literature has been getting all the critical notice. It amounts to about the same thing. And whole areas of America find themselves essentially voiceless: writers who essay to be their voice are either diverted or neglected; many readers who look for themselves in contemporary books find nobody who even resembles them. They read what the reviewers and critics praise, and find it either strange or antipathetic. Sometimes it strikes them as sick. They venture to express their personal tastes and the knowing laugh at them.

Let me make an important qualification or distinction here, for fear I should sound like some Midwest regionalist or Southern Agrarian complaining that we are dominated by New York intellectuals. Edgar Lee Masters and Vachel Lindsay could feel that way around 1920, a Southern Agrarian such as Donald Davidson feels that way to this day. But it is not the mere centralization of publishing and the critical establishment in New York, and it is not intellectuals as such (though they are sometimes ignorant and sometimes arrogant) that I am speaking of. There have been times when even with publishing concentrated in New York, other groups have succeeded in capturing the critical establishment almost as thoroughly as it is captured now. There have been times when little regional magazines actually pulled off a revolution. In the 1910s *Poetry* and the *Little Review*, both published in Chicago, had more weight in promoting modernism than a hatful of periodicals ten times their size and circulation. There was a time in the 1930s when the knowing went not to New York but to the *Southern Review*, the *Kenyon Quarterly*, the *Sewanee Review*, and other magazines for what was then the yeasty and rising dope. Whether the fashion happens to be Midwestern realism or Imagist revolt or Agrarian sectionalism or urban intellectualism is less important than that avenues be kept open for other manners and other preoccupations, and for the kinds of literary performance, whether experimental or traditional, that may offer outlets to bottled-up writers and frustrated readers.

This is a big lack, and it has been apparent to many for a long time. First novelists have trouble even getting reviewed, much less praised, and in consequence sometimes try any startling or shocking gimmick to attract notice. The reviewing journals dwindle and fade, the *Saturday Review of Literature* becomes the *Saturday Review* and cuts its book coverage by two-thirds, and the *New York Times Book Review* grows so stodgy that people all over the country complain, and during a *Times* strike the rival *New York Review of Books* is born—to many, a hopeful event. But week by week the *New York Review of Books* shows itself in turn to be dominated by a group, and seems more and more the journalistic brother of the *Partisan Review*; and even if it were as good as we all hoped it might be, its policy has consistently been to give large space to a few books, and leave out of notice a great number. We need some sort of widely disseminated and influential journal like the *London Times Literary Supplement*, with its brief, responsible, and numerous notices of new books.

What all this comes to is that the writer, who must write

out of his special culture because it is all he has, can hardly write *for* his special culture alone, unless it happens to be the fashion of the moment. He must write, eventually, for the man in the armchair, being aware of him without very seriously trying to define him. He will turn out, I suspect, to be someone very like the writer himself, and in this sense it may be said that a writer writes to please himself and lets the audience find him. Yet the man in the armchair (or the lady in the chaise longue) is someone *other*, too, and that makes all the difference. A writer is a man in search of an audience just as surely as he is a man in search of form; and just as form is at its best a *discovery*, something arrived at through the trial and error of creation, so the reader himself is a sort of discovery, and often a pleasant one. And despite the standardization of the reviewing media, despite the temporary suppression of whole areas of the American land and experience and people, that discovery may be made if the book has anything to say. I have said somewhere else that a work of literature is not primarily a gem, but a lens, a thing to look through, and that one thing we get by looking through it is a sense of intense acquaintance with the best in the man who wrote it. The meeting of writer and reader is an intimate act, and it *properly* takes place in private.

A NOTE ON TECHNIQUE

To MAKE A NOVEL, Dumas said, you need a passion and four walls. He might have added that to make a passion you need people in a bind, a situation full of love, hate, ambition, longing, some tension that cries to be resolved. A beginning writer may have trouble finding his real situation—he may have only clues, characters, a place, an atmosphere, the haunting association of ideas in his mind. In a novel he may even be able to grope for the situation through his first chapters (though one formula for the novel proposed by the late Bernard DeVoto was to throw away the first five chapters and start with number six), but in a short story the situation must be located at once, for even more than a novel, a short story must start off running, must begin on a rolling slope, as near the end as possible.

Because no situation can exist apart from what brought it about and what it leads to—apart, that is, from its antecedents and its consequences—the writer will be led both forward and backward from his germinal knot of tension. He must deal at least a little with the past, which in fictional technique is called *summary* or *exposition*; and he must deal with the dramatic present, which is called *scene*. Summary and scene are all there is to fiction, but neither is simple.

To make a scene is to put your characters onstage and let them act out their own story. The point of view may not be strictly objective—there may be some equivalent of the Stage Manager of *Our Town* lounging around somewhere—but any scene is essentially dramatic; it follows George M. Cohan's celebrated advice, "Don't tell 'em—show 'em." A scene must persuade us in all its aspects, which means that the characters must be credible and consistent; that the dialog must approximate real talk without being cluttered by real talk's monotony, fatuousness, and repetition; that the action must move in a direct line, without wanderings or irrelevancies, and that an internal logic must hold the scene together, beginning and middle and end; and that the setting must be sensuously realized and then never permitted to drop away and be forgotten. If any object is important enough to be mentioned, it should be put to some use. As Chekhov says, if you hang a gun on the wall at the beginning, it has to go off before the end. If there is a fireplace in a scene, characters should warm themselves by it, or lean on its mantel, as part of their stage business, their real-seeming.

One does not learn to do a job such as this by the old classroom method of practicing whole paragraphs of description, whole chunks of setting or characterization. The elements interweave; there are many balls to be kept in the air at once; a single paragraph may contain a fragment of action, a bit of dialog which by its content or its manner and tone characterizes the speaker, a sensuous perception of some detail of setting, a glance backward in memory, dialog, or external comment to pick up a meaningful bit of the past. Any page of fiction will have descriptive, narrative, dramatic, and expository writing all entangled. To make it all the more complicated, in modern fiction even the summary is likely to be worked into the scene.

There is reason why it should be, for by its very nature summary is inert. It has already happened, and so can have none of the excitement of what is dramatically happening now. Badly handled, it gives itself away by its lumbering use of the past perfect tense and by the weight of its blocks of dead stoppage while the past is gathered up. Well handled, summary can even achieve a kind of suspense, for suspense is gained primarily by keeping back essential information, by refusing to answer questions that arise in the reader's mind, and if a writer will remember never to explain too much, and when he does explain, to explain indirectly and a little at a time, he is not likely to bring his story to a grinding halt while the past perfect goes by in the other direction. Bring the summary in by the side door; keep her masked; she is an ugly girl with three left feet, and she will not do to dance with, but she can cook and keep house, and if you treat her well she will stay out of sight.

Now for a few rules of thumb; some of them repetitions:

1. Start in the middle of things; begin in motion.
2. Stay in motion by not letting the summary intrude; keep the summary feeding into the scene in hints and driblets, by what Ibsen called the "uncovering" technique.
3. Never explain too much; a reader is offended if he cannot

participate and use his mind and imagination, and a story loses much of its suspense the moment everything is explained.

4. Stay out of your story; pick a point of view and (especially in the short story) stay with it. Nobody has less right in your story than yourself.

5. Don't show off in your style. The writing should match the characters and the situation, not you. This applies as well to obscenity and profanity as to other matters. Where character and situation call for them, they belong; elsewhere they may be a sign that the author is trying to catch someone's attention.

6. Nothing is to be gained, except a breaking of the dramatic illusion, by attempts to find substitutes for the word "said" in dialog tags. "Said" is a colorless word that disappears; elegant variations show up.

7. Stopping a story is as hard as saying goodnight. Learn to do it cleanly, without leftovers or repetitions.

"GOIN' TO TOWN":
AN OBJECT LESSON

ALL I WANT TO DO THIS EVENING is read a story and talk a little about it, and in the process say a word about the nature and validity of fiction.

Fiction has never been without its detractors. The New England Puritans thought it was dangerous lies, and some people still do, and some fiction still is. "Practical" Americans, mainly male, tend to look on fiction as an innocuous frill, a suitable pastime for women's clubs, part of the interior decoration of life but not of its architecture, and some fiction is. Some writers write, and some readers read, not to confront or examine their lives but to escape from them into a world where men are nobler and sexier, and women more beautiful, than in our nine-to-five world, and where male or female adventures, rape and murder, gang bangs and gang killings and space journeys, enliven with their fantasy our otherwise dull days.

And one kind of critics, the deconstructionist magi of Yale and its colonies, have declared themselves superior to fiction, and to literature in general. It is a joke. Both it and its makers are themselves fictions, mosaics of culturally constructed myths, fragments of previous texts and stereotyped values, phatic verbiage, reverberations of old delusions, echoes of echoes. The delight of these critics is to show what shopworn stuff literature is made of and what shoddy tricks it employs. They destroy their own justification for being, and before long, like the snake that took hold of its own tail and swallowed itself, they will vanish like all the other oversubtle and scholastic aberrations of history. Perhaps, once we have had them, we will be immune, as we are after having had measles.

The point is, our fiction—what we write and what we read—is likely to be as frivolous or as serious as our lives are. If we never examine our lives, we are not likely to get much out of fiction that makes such examination its function. Sure fiction is made of shopworn materials: human lives. Sure there are echoes in it, as there are in life, from a long way back. There has been something like human consciousness in the world for a couple of million years, or what is Robert Bly beating his chest and his drum about?

Because I tend to take life seriously, what I like about it and what I don't, I believe in fiction, not only in its do-ability but in its importance. For the writer, whose life is as often as not a mess, it can clean up a murky and littered mind as snails clean up a fish tank. And at its best it leaves behind a purified residue, an artifact, something shaped and created and capable of communicating whatever wisdom it has arrived at. Even a deconstructionist could benefit from it if he would.

The story I will read is called "Goin' to Town," an old one. It was published in the *Atlantic Monthly* for June 1940, and later used as a chapter in the novel *The Big Rock Candy*

Mountain. It is not a story in the modern vein. I choose it not because it reveals the world to our suddenly unsealed eyes, or because it demonstrates anything about the changing form of the short story, or because I think it is the best thing I ever wrote, but because it is simple and undevious and unambiguous. I know what experience it comes from, I know what's in it, I know why I wrote it, I know what I got out of writing it. As well as any story I might have picked, it can be used to substantiate my faith that fictionizing is an essential function of the mind and emotions—that reality is not fully reality *until* it has been fictionized.

❑ ❑ ❑

GOIN' TO TOWN

After the night's rain the yard was spongy and soft under the boy's bare feet. He stood at the edge of the packed dooryard in the flat thrust of sunrise, looking at the ground washed clean and smooth and trackless, feeling the cool firm mud under his toes. Experimentally he lifted his right foot and put it down in a new place, pressed, picked it up again to look at the neat imprint of straight edge and curving instep and the five round dots of toes. The air was so fresh that he sniffed at it as he would have sniffed at the smell of cinnamon.

Lifting his head backward, he saw how the prairie beyond the fireguard looked darker than in dry times, healthier with green-brown tints, smaller and more intimate somehow than it did when the heat waves crawled over scorched grass and carried the horizons backward into dim and unseeable distances. And standing in the yard above his one clean sharp footprint, feeling his own verticality in all that spread of horizontal land, he sensed how the prairie shrank on this morning and how he himself grew. He was immense. A little jump would crack his head on the sky; a few strides would take him to any horizon.

His eyes turned south, into the low south sky, cloudless, almost colorless in the strong light. Just above the brown line of the horizon, faint as a watermark on pale blue paper, was the wavering tracery of the mountains, tenuous and far off, but today accessible for the first time. His mind had played among those ghostly summits for uncountable lost hours; today, in a few strides, they were his. And more: under the shadow of those peaks, under those Bearpaws that he and his mother privately called the Mountains of the Moon, was Chinook; and in Chinook, on this Fourth of July, were the band, the lemonade stands, the crowds, the parade, the ball game, the fireworks that his mind had hungered toward in anticipation for three weeks.

His shepherd pup lay watching, belly down on the damp ground. In a gleeful spasm the boy stooped down to flap the pup's ears, then bent and spun like an Indian in a war dance while the wide-mouthed dog raced

around him. And when his father came to the door in
his undershirt, yawning, running a hand up the back of
his head and through his hair, peering out from
gummed eyes to see how the weather looked, the boy
watched him, and his voice was one deep breathing re-
lief from yesterday's rainy fear.

"It's clear as a bell," he said.

His father yawned again, clopped his jaws, rubbed
his eyes, mumbled something from a mouth furry with
sleep. He stood on the doorstep scratching himself com-
fortably, looking down at the boy and the dog.

"Gonna be hot," he said slyly. "Might be too hot to
drive."

"Aw, Pa!"

"Gonna be a scorcher. Melt you right down to axle
grease riding in that car."

The boy regarded him doubtfully, saw the lurking
sly droop of his mouth. "Aw, we are too going!"

At his father's laugh he burst from his immobility
like a sprinter starting, raced one complete circle of the
house with the dog after him. When he flew around
past his father again his voice trailed out behind him at
the corner of the house. "Gonna feed the hens," he said.
His father looked after him, scratched himself, laughed
suddenly, and went back indoors.

Through chores and breakfast the boy moved with the
dream of a day's rapture haunting his eyes, but that did
not keep him from swift and agile helpfulness. He

didn't even wait for commands. He scrubbed himself twice, slicked down his hair, hunted up clean clothes, wiped the mud from his shoes with a wet rag and put them on. While his mother packed the shoe box of lunch he stood at her elbows proffering aid. He flew to stow things in the topless old Ford. He got a cloth and polished the brass radiator. Once or twice, jumping around to help, he looked up to catch his parents watching him, or looking at each other with the knowing, smiling expression in the eyes that said they were calling each other's attention to him.

"Just like a race horse," his father said once, and the boy felt foolish, swaggered, twisted his mouth down in a leer, said "Awww!" But in a moment he was hustling them again. They ought to get going, with fifty miles to drive. And long before they were ready he was standing beside the Ford, licked and immaculate and so excited that his feet jumped him up and down without his volition or knowledge.

It was eight o'clock before his father came out, lifted off the front seat, poked the flat stick down into the gas tank, pulled it out again dripping. "Pretty near full," he said. "If we're gonna drive up to the mountains we better take a can along, though. Fill that two-gallon one with the spout."

The boy ran, dug the can out of the shed, filled it from the spigot of the sixty-gallon drum that stood on a plank support to the north of the farmhouse. When he came back, his left arm stuck straight out and the can knocking against his legs, his mother was settling herself into the back seat among the parcels and water bags.

"Goodness!" she said. "This is the first time I've been the first ready since I don't know when. I should think you'd have got all this done last night."

"Plenty time." The father stood looking down at the boy, grinning. "All right, race horse. You want to go to this shindig, you better hop in."

The boy was up into the front seat like a squirrel. His father walked around in front of the car. "Okay," he said. "You look sharp now. When she kicks over, switch her onto magneto and pull the spark down."

The boy said nothing. He looked upon the car, as his father did, with respect and a little awe. They didn't use it much, and starting it was a ritual like a fire drill. The father unscrewed the four-eared brass plug, looked down into the radiator, screwed the cap back on, and bent to take hold of the crank. "Watch it now," he said.

The boy felt the gentle heave of the springs, up and down, as his father wound the crank. He heard the gentle hiss in the bowels of the engine as the choke wire was pulled out, and his nostrils filled with the strong, volatile odor of gasoline. Over the slope of the radiator his father's brown strained face lifted up. "Is she turned on all right?"

"Yup. She's on battery."

"Must of flooded her. Have to let her rest a minute."

They waited—and then after a few minutes the wavelike heaving of the springs again, the rise and fall of the blue shirt and bent head over the radiator, the sighing swish of the choke, a stronger smell of gasoline. The motor had not even coughed.

The two voices came simultaneously from the car. "What's the matter with it?"

His brow puckered in an intent and serious scowl, the father stood blowing mighty breaths. "Son of a gun," he said. Coming around, he pulled at the switch to make sure it was clear over, adjusted the spark and gas levers. A fine mist of sweat made his face shine like oiled leather in the sun.

"There isn't anything really wrong with it, is there?" the mother said, and her voice wavered uncertainly on the edge of fear.

"I don't see how there could be," he said. "She's always started right off, and she was running all right when I drove her in here."

The boy looked at his mother where she sat erect among the things in the seat. She looked all dressed up, a flowered dress, a hat with hard red varnished cherries on it pinned to her red hair. For a moment she sat, stiff and nervous. "What'll you have to do?" she said.

"I don't know. Look into the motor."

"Well, I guess I'll get in out of the sun while you do it," she said, and, opening the door, she fumbled her way out of the clutter.

The boy felt her exodus like a surrender, a betrayal.

If they didn't hurry up they'd miss the parade. In one motion he bounced out of the car. "Gee whiz!" he said. "Let's do something. We got to get started."

"Keep your shirt on," his father grunted. Lifting the hood, he bent his head inside, studying the engine. His hand went out to test wires, wiggle spark-plug connections, make tentative pulls at the choke. The weakly hinged hood slipped and came down across his wrist, and he swore, pushing it back. "Get me the pliers," he said.

For ten minutes he probed and monkeyed. "Might be the spark plugs," he said. "She don't seem to be getting any fire through her."

The mother, sitting on a box in the shade, smoothed her flowered voile dress nervously. "Will it take long?"

"Half-hour."

"Any day but this!" she said. "I don't see why you didn't make sure last night."

He breathed through his nose and bent over the engine again. "Don't go laying on any blame," he said. "It was raining last night."

One by one the plugs came out, were squinted at, scraped with a knife blade, the gap tested with a thin dime. The boy stood on one foot, then on the other, time pouring like a flood of uncatchable silver dollars through his hands. He kept looking at the sun, estimating how much time there was left. If they got it started right away they might still make it for the parade, but it would be close. Maybe they'd drive right up the street while the parade was on, and be part of it. . . .

"Is she ready?" he said.

"Pretty quick."

He wandered over by his mother, and she reached out and put an arm around his shoulders, hugging him quickly. "Well, anyway we'll get there for the band and the ball game and the fireworks," he said. "If she doesn't start till noon we c'n make it for those."

"Sure," she said. "Pa'll get it going in a minute. We won't miss anything, hardly."

"You ever seen skyrockets, Ma?"

"Once."

"Are they fun?"

"Wonderful," she said. "Just like a million stars, all colors, exploding all at once."

His feet took him back to his father, who straightened up with a belligerent grunt. "Now!" he said. "If the sucker doesn't start now . . ."

And once more the heaving of the springs, the groaning of the turning engine, the hiss of choke. He tried short, sharp half-turns, as if to catch the motor off guard. Then he went back to the stubborn laboring spin. The back of his blue shirt was stained darkly, the curving dikes of muscle along the spine's hollow showing cleanly where the cloth stuck. Over and over, heaving, stubborn at first, then furious, until he staggered back panting.

"God damn!" he said. "What you suppose is the matter with the damn thing?"

"She didn't even cough once," the boy said, and, staring up at his father's face full of angry bafflement, he felt the cold fear touch him. What if it didn't start at all? What if they never got to any of it? What if, all ready to go, they had to turn around and unload the Ford and not even get out of the yard? His mother came over and they stood close together, looking at the Ford and avoiding each other's eyes.

"Maybe something got wet last night," she said.

"Well, it's had plenty time to dry out," said his father.

"Isn't there anything else you could try?"

"We can jack up the hind wheel, I guess. But there's no damn reason we ought to have to."

"Well, if you have to, you'll have to," she said briskly. "After planning it for three weeks we can't just get stuck like this. Can we, son?"

His answer was mechanical, his eyes steady on his father. "Sure not," he said.

The father opened his mouth to say something, saw the boy's lugubrious face, and shut his lips again. Without a word he pulled off the seat and got out the jack.

The sun climbed steadily while they jacked up one hind wheel and blocked the car carefully so that it wouldn't run over anybody when it started. The boy helped, and when they were ready again he sat in the front seat so full of hope and fear that his whole body was one taut concentration. His father stooped, his cheek pressed against the radiator as a milker's cheek touches the flank of a cow. His shoulder dropped, jerked up. Nothing. Another jerk. Nothing. Then he was rolling in a furious spasm of energy, the wet dark back of his shirt rising and falling. And inside the motor only the futile swish of the choke and the half sound, half feel of cavernous motion as the crankshaft turned over. The Ford bounced on its springs as if the front wheels were coming off the ground on every upstroke. Then it stopped, and the boy's father was hanging on the radiator, breathless, dripping wet, swearing. "Son of a dirty, lousy, stinking, corrupted . . ."

The boy, his eyes dark, stared from his father's angry wet face to his mother's, pinched with worry. The pup lay down in the shade and put his head on his paws. "Gee whiz," the boy said. "Gee whiz!" He looked at the sky, and the morning was half gone.

His shoulders jerking with anger, the father threw the crank halfway across the yard and took a step or two toward the house. "The hell with the damn thing!"

"Harry, you can't!"

He stopped, glared at her, took an oblique look at the boy, bared his teeth in an irresolute, silent swearword. "Well, God, if it won't go!"

"Maybe if you hitched the horses to it," she said.

His laugh was short and choppy. "That'd be fine!" he said. "Why don't we just hitch up and let the team haul this damned old boat into Chinook?"

"But we've got to get it started! Why wouldn't it be all right to let them pull it around? You push it sometimes on a hill and it starts."

He looked at the boy again, jerked his eyes away with an exasperated gesture, as if he held the boy somehow accountable. The boy stared, mournful, defeated, ready to cry, and his father's head swung back unwillingly. Then abruptly he winked, mopped his head and neck, and grinned. "Think you want to go, uh?"

The boy nodded. "All right!" his father's voice snapped crisply. "Fly up in the pasture and get the team. Hustle!"

On the high lope the boy was off up the coulee bank. Just down under the lip of the swale, a quarter-mile west, the bay backs of the horses and the black dot of the colt showed. Usually he ran circumspectly across that pasture, because of the cactus, but now he flew. With shoes it was all right, and even without shoes he would have run—across burnouts, over stretches so undermined with gopher holes that sometimes he broke through to the ankle, staggering. Skimming over patches of cactus, soaring over a badger hole, plunging down into the coulee and up the other side, he ran as if bears were after him. The black colt, spotting him, hoisted his tail and took off in a spectacular, stiff-legged sprint across the flats, but the bays merely lifted their heads to watch him. He slowed, came up walking, laid a hand on the mare's neck and untied the looped halter rope. She stood for him while he scrambled and wriggled and kicked his way to her back, and then they were off, the mare in an easy lope, the gelding trotting after, the colt stopping his wild showoff career and wobbling hastily and ignominiously after his departing mother.

They pulled up before the Ford, the boy sliding off to throw the halter rope to his father. "Shall I get the harness?" he said, and before anyone could answer he was off running, to come back lugging one heavy harness, tugs trailing little furrows in the damp bare earth. He dropped it, turned to run again, his breath laboring in his lungs. "I'll get the other'n," he said.

With a short, almost incredulous laugh his father looked at his mother and shook his head before he threw the harness on the mare. When the second one came he laid it over the gelding, pushed against the heavy shoulder to get the horse into place. The gelding resisted, pranced a little, got a curse and a crack with the rope across his nose, jerked back and trembled and lifted his feet nervously, and set one shod hoof on his owner's instep. The father, unstrung by the hurry and the heat and the labor and the exasperation of a morning when nothing went right, kicked the horse savagely in the belly. "Get in there, you damned big blundering ox! Back! Back, you bastard! Whoa! Whoa, now!"

With a heavy rope for a towline he hitched the now-skittish team to the axle. Without a word he stooped and lifted the boy to the mare's back. "All right," he said, and his face relaxed in a quick grin. "This is where we start her. Ride 'em around in a circle, not too fast."

Then he climbed into the Ford, turned on the switch to magneto, fussed with the levers. "Let her go!" he said.

The boy kicked the mare ahead, twisting as he rode to watch the Ford heave forward as a tired, heavy man heaves to his feet, begin rolling after him, lurching on the uneven ground, jerking and kicking and making

growling noises when his father let the emergency
brake off and put it in gear. The horses settled as the
added pull came on them, flattened into their collars,
swung in a circle, bumped each other, skittered. The
mare reared, and the boy shut his eyes and clung. When
he came down, her leg was entangled in the towline
and his father was climbing cursing out of the Ford to
straighten it out. His father was mad again, and yelled
at him, "Keep 'em apart! There ain't any tongue. You
got to keep Dick kicked over on his own side."

And again the start, the flattening into the collars,
the snapping tight of the tugs under his legs. This time
it went smoothly, the Ford galloped after the team in
lumbering, plunging jerks. The mare's eyes rolled
white, and she broke into a trot, pulling the gelding after her. Desperately the boy clung to the knotted and
shortened reins, his ears alert for the grumble of the
Ford starting behind him. The pup ran beside the team
yapping in a high, falsetto, idiot monotone, crazy with
excitement.

They made three complete circles of the back yard
between house and chicken coop before the boy looked
back again. "Won't she start?" he shouted. He saw his
father rigid behind the wheel, heard his ripping burst
of swearwords, saw him bend and glare down into the
mysterious innards of the engine through the pulled-up
floorboards. Guiding the car with one hand, he fumbled
down below, one glaring eye just visible over the cowl.

"Shall I stop?" the boy shouted. Excitement and
near-despair made his voice a tearful scream.

But his father's wild arm waved him on. "Go on, go on! Gallop 'em! Pull the guts out of this thing. Run 'em, run 'em!"

And the galloping—the furious, mud-flinging, rolling-eyed galloping around the circle already rutted like a road, the Ford, now in savagely held low, growling and surging and plowing behind; the mad yapping of the dog, the erratic scared bursts of runaway from the colt, the mother in sight briefly for a quarter of each circle, her hands to her mouth and her eyes hurt, and behind him in the Ford his father in a strangling rage, yelling him on, his lips back over his teeth and his face purple.

Until finally they stopped, the horses blown, the boy white and tearful and still, the father dangerous with unexpended wrath. The boy slipped off, his lip bitten between his teeth, not crying now but ready to at any moment, the corners of his eyes prickling with it, and his teeth tight on his misery. His father climbed over the side of the car and stood looking as if he wanted to tear the thing apart with his bare hands.

Shoulders sagging, tears trembling to fall, his jaw aching with the need to cry, the boy started toward his mother. As he came near his father he looked up, their eyes met, and he saw his father's blank with impotent rage. Dull hopelessness swallowed him. Not any of it, his mind said. Not even any of it—no parade, no ball game, no band, no fireworks. No lemonade or ice cream or paper horns or firecrackers. No close sight of the mountains that throughout every summer called like a legend from his horizons. No trip, no adventure—none of it, nothing.

Everything he was feeling was in that one still look. In spite of him his lip trembled, and he choked off a sob, his eyes on his father's face, on the brows pulled down and the eyes narrowing.

"Well, don't blubber!" his father shouted at him. "Don't stand there looking at me as if it was me that was keeping you from your picnic!"

"I can't—help it," the boy said, and with a kind of terror he felt the grief swelling up, overwhelming him, driving the voice out of him in a wail. Through the blur of his crying he saw the convulsive tightening of his father's face, and then all the fury of a maddening morning concentrated itself in a swift backhand blow that knocked the boy staggering.

He bawled aloud, from pain, from surprise, from outrage, from pure desolation, and ran to bury his face in his mother's skirts. From that muffled sanctuary he heard her angry voice. "No," she said. "It won't do any good to try to make up to him now. Go on away somewhere till he gets over it."

She rocked him against her, but the voice she had for his father was bitter with anger. "As if he wasn't hurt enough already!" she said.

He heard the heavy, quick footsteps going away, and for a long time he lay crying into the voile flowers. And when he had cried himself out, and had listened apathetically to his mother's soothing promises that they would go in the first chance they got, go to the mountains, have a picnic under some waterfall, maybe be able to find a ball game going on in town, some Saturday—— when he had listened and become quiet, wanting to believe it but not believing it at all, he went inside to take off his good clothes and his shoes and put on his old overalls again.

It was almost noon when he came out to stand in the front yard looking southward toward the impossible land where the Mountains of the Moon lifted above the plains, and where, in the town at the foot of the peaks, crowds would now be eating picnic lunches, drinking pop, getting ready to go out to the ball field and watch heroes in real uniforms play ball. The band would be braying now from a bunting-wrapped stand, kids would be tossing firecrackers, playing in a cool grove. . . .

In the still heat his face went sorrowful and defeated, and his eyes searched the horizon for the telltale watermark. But there was nothing but waves of heat crawling and lifting like invisible flames; the horizon was a blurred and writhing flatness where earth and sky met in an indistinct band of haze. This morning two strides would have taken him there; now it was gone.

Looking down, he saw at his feet the clean footprint that he had made in the early morning. Aimlessly he put his right foot down and pressed. The mud was drying, but in a low place he found a spot that would still take an imprint. Very carefully, as if he were performing some ritual for his life, he went around, stepping and leaning, stepping and leaning, until he had a circle six feet in diameter of delicately exact footprints, straight edge and curving instep and the five round dots of toes.

❑ ❑ ❑

Most readers would assume, correctly, that this story reflects an experience of the author himself. I spent six years of my childhood in Saskatchewan, and more than six years resenting my father's impatience and violence. When I wrote the story, twenty-three years after that blasted Fourth of July, the disappointment itself had long since faded—it faded, actually, within a day or two. But the resentment did not fade, perhaps because it was fed by other similar incidents, and as a grown man, my father dead, I was still asking myself what sort of person it is who, when balked by circumstances, takes out his frustration on the principal victim of those circumstances, the one who deserves sympathy, not a crack on the head. I was still sorry for myself, and I was making a moral indictment, getting even for what I felt was both an injustice and an unkindness. Writing this story was like getting a foxtail out of a sock.

But I think hoarded resentment was not the only reason my subconscious sent up this story from the cellar. There was regret and guilt as well as resentment involved. As I recreated that bad day on the homestead in 1917 I began to realize that I was not only outraged by my father's act, I was desolated by it, I wanted it not to have happened, I wanted to admire him and be loved by him, I wanted not to have offended him with my crybabyishness, I wanted to be the sort of son he could be proud of. Getting even was only one impulse, and a not very attractive one, of what moved me. I also found myself wanting to understand, to make a reconciliation of some kind, to soothe my own anger and unease, to lay to rest his troubled and troubling ghost.

That is to say, I was entering on a course of self-therapy, which is at least as difficult as the hired kind. As it turned out, this story didn't do the job. Even the long novel, *The Big Rock Candy Mountain*, which contains a half dozen episodes of this kind, didn't do it. I had to come back years later with another novel, *Recapitulation*, before the past seemed to me healed.

What I am saying, to no one's surprise, is that one of the reasons people write fiction is to heal themselves by making an improved model of some aspect of their lives. A story can zipper up old wounds in the person who writes it. And it is cheaper than other methods. When I was writing *The Big Rock Candy Mountain* I was teaching at Harvard, and a Cambridge literary lady, seeing these fragments of my childhood in magazines, asked me seriously if I thought I should write so many unhappy stories about childhood. Was it *healthy*? I didn't know, but I told her truthfully that if I wrote them I could get X-hundred dollars apiece for them, and if I told them to a psychoanalyst they would cost me twenty-five dollars an hour. That was a joke, but only sort of.

Notice that "Goin' to Town" is not a first-person lament. The boy is not myself, but another eight-year-old called "he." An old rule of storytelling says that the first person provides an eyewitness immediacy, and the wisdom of the couch says that healing depends on ventilating the most personal items in the mental closet. Why didn't I tell this as personal experience and get the maximum effect out of it?

Two reasons, both of them dictated from the cellar of the subconscious where reality waits to be civilized into fiction.

First, though the first person guarantees immediacy, it also risks the taint of self-pity. And I was already aware that self-pity was part of my motivation. Without any conscious decision, without my even being aware I was doing it, I changed "I" to "he" out of some instinctive wariness about self-exposure. Perhaps I was remembering Robert Frost, who also had a violent father and knew the problem. He told me once that we should always write what happened to someone else as if it had happened to us, and what happened to us as if it had happened to someone else. That way, we get immediacy for places where it is needed, and a cooler distance on people and events that come too close.

Moreover, at the same time that I was pushing the episode off at arm's length and gaining at least the illusion of objectivity, I was also cleaning up the action. This is not unsorted memory that comes out on the page, but something selected, arranged, given emphasis in one place, muted in another. By no means everything I remember about that Fourth of July morning is in the story. I remember that my mother mislaid something, and we took the house apart looking for it so we wouldn't be without it on the trip to town. I remember that while we were hunting that lost object, whatever it was, a hawk struck a pullet in the yard, and we rushed out to chase the hawk away and rescue the poor chicken, its crop torn open and its heart, as I held the bird in my hands, pounding like an engine. My mother got needle and thread and sewed the crop up, and we turned the pullet loose and watched her stagger around, and sit down with half-spread wings and open beak. By the time we gave up on the Ford, she was dead. That was all perfectly good homestead detail, part of the personal experience, but I used none of it. None of it belonged in the story.

What belonged in the story was only the big dream of the Fourth of July, the ball game, the fireworks, the lemonade stands; the preparation for all that wonder as imagined by an eight-year-old who hadn't seen another child for three weeks and had never seen anything of the big world he imagines; the fear that is introduced when the Ford won't start, and grows as every new effort to start it fails through what becomes a serial ordeal; and the final disappointment, defeat, the backhanded blow. That is all that belongs in this story; I hope that is all that's there.

As I have already indicated, this is very different from the couch. Though it may have purgative effects, a story is not simply the result of reverse peristalsis, it's not a spiritual emetic. There is some kind of direction going on here, and don't ask me where it comes from, whether from some critic in the writer's pilot house or some dark preprogrammed demand of the story itself. Most writers don't want to investigate that mystery. Once when a pair of very distinguished psychologists interested in the creative process came to my Stanford class and asked for volunteers to be hypnotized so their creative processes could be examined, the whole class turned pale and all but fled the room.

Direction, wherever it comes from. Something is being made, experience is being converted from its raw state into a state more shapely and meaningful. At least when one is both the patient and the healer, healing comes about not through mere ventilation but through conversion and creation. Order has been imposed on the chaos of experience, sensation, and memory, and it is the order that heals. It is also the order that makes the converted experience accessible to readers. Instead of a shapeless personal experience, a wilderness full of brambles and poison oak, a story is a designed park, with flower beds, walks, keep-off-the-grass signs, and comfort stations. If, as Henry Adams said, chaos is the law of nature and order the dream of man, then fiction is nearer to the heart's desire than raw experience is, and its meanings more comprehensible.

Short stories being what they are, able to take a character or action or relationship to the corner but not around it, my effort to get some reconciliation into "Goin' to Town" didn't come to much. Neither is there as much about the setting, which was immensely impressive to me as a child, as I would have liked. Actually it took me three stories to do everything that I wanted this one to do. The setting, the lonely, wild, beautiful prairie with the dream of mountains at its edge, I concentrated into a little story called "Bugle Song," which just precedes "Goin' to Town" in *The Big Rock Candy Mountain*; and the reconciliation which is only hinted at in "Goin' to Town" I made the subject of another story, "Two Rivers," which immediately follows it in the novel. In this last story, the Ford starts, the picnic to the mountains comes off, the father is jovial and humorous, they have adventures, the whole day from sunup to sundown is smooth and happy. I have to admit, though, that it never happened: we never did get to the mountains all the time we lived out there. At least the imaginary trip satisfied something that wanted to be satisfied. If you can't remember it, make it up. Also, those mountains I described weren't the Bearpaws.

At the risk of talking one small story to death, I want to say a word about its form, the sense of closure and completeness that I hope it has and that I believe every satisfactory story must have. As anybody can testify, experience is a continuous shower, without beginnings or endings. It ravels off from previous experiences and frays off into new ones. Because the record of any experience is not complete without a thinking pause after it, and because most readers have a short attention span, the writer's job is to contrive a positive conclusion that will pass for an ending of the limited segment of life the story covers. In a plotted story there is a rising action, a series of complications, a climax, a denouement. Somebody or something wins or loses, lives or dies. That is what Hemingway had in mind when he said that all stories end in death—there is no other ending that really ends anything. So we must contrive little symbolic deaths that *seem* to end something, and we must be careful when we do it; for beginnings and endings, Chekhov said, are the places where writers are most inclined to lie.

Here, there is no real death. There is only the death of a childish dream, and perhaps a boy's trust in his father. So how, in practical terms, do I close this episode off? Is the mere disappointment enough? Do we end, without further comment, with that crack on the head? Or does the story go on until the boy goes forlornly back into the house to take off his town clothes and his shoes and put his old overalls back on? I considered both of those, and wasn't quite satisfied with either. Eventually I looked back to the beginning, to where the boy tried out his footprint in the muddy yard. At the beginning that print was triumphant, it meant an exhilarating sense of identity and power. A little jump would crack his head on the sky, a few strides would take him to any horizon. Like Anasazi handprints on a cliff, that footprint said, "I am I, and I am Somebody."

That was in the morning. Now it is afternoon, the dream is dead, the boy is bruised, confused, depressed. So some voice from down in the basement where these things are decided told me to return him to that footprint, but in a different mood. Make some later footprints, but make them different. What I did was make them go around in a circle. They don't assert identity; they make a kind of wall or fence within which this lonesome farm kid is imprisoned. The far horizons, the mountains of the moon, the dreamed-of wonders of Chinook, Montana, are shut out; the spirit is isolated and shut in. The thing that most recommended the use of the structural symbol of the footprints, which enclose the story as if in parentheses, is that they say what they mean without having to say it out loud. They let me end the story with a mood-closing as well as an action-closing statement. Structural symbols aren't always available; the device won't always work. One is lucky when it does.

I confess that I think myself lucky most of the time, lucky whenever a story is working through the processing plant from feeling or memory or idea toward its becoming as a fiction. The best times I know are the times when some raw crystal of experience, my own or something I have observed, is being ground down and faceted and polished so that it reflects light and meaning. What the storytelling impulse adds to experience is at least the illusion that one is in control, and providing direction. Considering how life often goes, that is a very comforting illusion. It may be the one that makes life possible. Certainly it is the thing that tells me I am lucky in my profession. I wouldn't trade it for any other in the world.

FOR THE BEST IN PAPERBACKS, LOOK FOR THE

In every corner of the world, on every subject under the sun, Penguin represents quality and variety—the very best in publishing today.

For complete information about books available from Penguin—including Penguin Classics, Penguin Compass, and Puffins—and how to order them, write to us at the appropriate address below. Please note that for copyright reasons the selection of books varies from country to country.

In the United States: Please write to *Penguin Putnam Inc., P.O. Box 12289 Dept. B, Newark, New Jersey 07101-5289* or call 1-800-788-6262.

In the United Kingdom: Please write to *Dept. EP, Penguin Books Ltd, Bath Road, Harmondsworth, West Drayton, Middlesex UB7 0DA.*

In Canada: Please write to *Penguin Books Canada Ltd, 10 Alcorn Avenue, Suite 300, Toronto, Ontario M4V 3B2.*

In Australia: Please write to *Penguin Books Australia Ltd, P.O. Box 257, Ringwood, Victoria 3134.*

In New Zealand: Please write to *Penguin Books (NZ) Ltd, Private Bag 102902, North Shore Mail Centre, Auckland 10.*

In India: Please write to *Penguin Books India Pvt Ltd, 11 Panchsheel Shopping Centre, Panchsheel Park, New Delhi 110 017.*

In the Netherlands: Please write to *Penguin Books Netherlands bv, Postbus 3507, NL-1001 AH Amsterdam.*

In Germany: Please write to *Penguin Books Deutschland GmbH, Metzlerstrasse 26, 60594 Frankfurt am Main.*

In Spain: Please write to *Penguin Books S. A., Bravo Murillo 19, 1° B, 28015 Madrid.*

In Italy: Please write to *Penguin Italia s.r.l., Via Benedetto Croce 2, 20094 Corsico, Milano.*

In France: Please write to *Penguin France, Le Carré Wilson, 62 rue Benjamin Baillaud, 31500 Toulouse.*

In Japan: Please write to *Penguin Books Japan Ltd, Kaneko Building, 2-3-25 Koraku, Bunkyo-Ku, Tokyo 112.*

In South Africa: Please write to *Penguin Books South Africa (Pty) Ltd, Private Bag X14, Parkview, 2122 Johannesburg.*